T0221635

Cambridge Elements ≡

Elements in Publishing and Book Culture
edited by
Samantha Rayner
University College London
Leah Tether
University of Bristol

ARE BOOKS STILL "DIFFERENT"?

Literature as Culture and Commodity in a Digital Age

Caroline Koegler
University of Münster

Corinna Norrick-Rühl
University of Münster

CAMBRIDGE
UNIVERSITY PRESS

CAMBRIDGE
UNIVERSITY PRESS

Shaftesbury Road, Cambridge CB2 8EA, United Kingdom

One Liberty Plaza, 20th Floor, New York, NY 10006, USA

477 Williamstown Road, Port Melbourne, VIC 3207, Australia

314–321, 3rd Floor, Plot 3, Splendor Forum, Jasola District Centre, New Delhi – 110025, India

103 Penang Road, #05–06/07, Visioncrest Commercial, Singapore 238467

Cambridge University Press is part of Cambridge University Press & Assessment, a department of the University of Cambridge.

We share the University's mission to contribute to society through the pursuit of education, learning and research at the highest international levels of excellence.

www.cambridge.org
Information on this title: www.cambridge.org/9781108987127

DOI: 10.1017/9781108982450

First published 2023

A catalogue record for this publication is available from the British Library.

ISBN 978-1-108-98712-7 Paperback
ISSN 2514-8524 (online)
ISSN 2514-8516 (print)

Are Books Still "Different"?

Literature as Culture and Commodity in a Digital Age

Elements in Publishing and Book Culture

DOI: 10.1017/9781108982450

First published online: February 2023

Caroline Koegler
University of Münster

Corinna Norrick-Rühl
University of Münster

Author for correspondence: Caroline Koegler, caroline.koegler@uni-muenster.de

ABSTRACT: The famous 1962 precedent at the Restrictive Practices Court of the United Kingdom, "Books are different," is still the reasoning behind many cultural policies around the world, building on long-standing assumptions surrounding "the book." As this suggests, the "difference" of the book as a unique form of cultural (rather than economic) production has acquired a powerful status. But are books still different? In (somewhat provocatively) asking this question from a network-oriented and interdisciplinary perspective (book studies/literary studies), this Element inquires into the notion of "difference" in relation to books. Challenging common notions of "bibliodiversity," it reconsiders the lack of diversity in the publishing industry. It also engages with the diversifying potentials of the digital literary sphere, offering a case study of Bernardine Evaristo's industry activities and activism. The Element concludes with thoughts on bookishness, affect, and networked practice. This title is also available as Open Access on Cambridge Core.

KEYWORDS: publishing, bibliodiversity, diversity, Bernardine Evaristo, digital literary sphere

ISBNs: 9781108987127 (PB), 9781108982450 (OC)

ISSNs: 2514-8524 (online), 2514-8516 (print)

Contents

1 Introduction: (Re-)thinking "Difference"

The year 2019 was an unprecedented year for literary prizes. The Nobel Prize for Literature had not been awarded due to a scandal in the Swedish Academy and the Booker, a prize awarded to the allegedly best novel of the literary season, was split between two winners in a surprising and controversial decision. As mentioned on the Booker's own website, not without spin and pathos, "Like a corpse in a zombie-flick, the old problem of split winners came back to life and an almighty ruckus ensued when Margaret Atwood and Bernardine Evaristo shared the prize."[1]

The zombie-esque split of the award not only brought together two authors to share one of the most prestigious book prizes worldwide but also clearly juxtaposed the logics of the literary market. *The Testaments* had been pushed into the market with a mind-boggling first print run of 500,000 in the USA alone – and within the first six days after publication, the American publisher Doubleday was able to print a new edition.[2] Part of the reason why *The Testaments* hit skyrocketing sales numbers was that it followed the serial adaptation of Atwood's dystopian novel *The Handmaid's Tale* (1985). The full-length film adaptation, released by MGM in 1990, had received mixed reviews. The series, available on Hulu since April 2017, found significant critical success and a wide reception in the wake of Donald Trump's election as President of the USA. Sales of *The Handmaid's Tale* reportedly increased by 60 percent in 2017 compared to the year prior.[3] Meanwhile, the marketing campaign for *The Testaments* was meticulously orchestrated and ran for almost a full year, from Margaret Atwood's first tweet announcing the book to a midnight launch at Waterstone's Piccadilly,

---

[1] The Booker Prizes, "The 2019 Booker Prize" (2019), https://thebookerprizes .com/the-booker-library/prize-years/2019.

[2] K. Mansfield, "Record-Breaking US Sales for the Testaments," *The Bookseller* (September 16, 2019), www.thebookseller.com/news/record-breaking-us-sales-testaments-1081431.

[3] K. Kilkenny, "Margaret Atwood Says Bulk of Hulu 'Handmaid's Tale' Profits Went to MGM," *The Hollywood Reporter* (February 2, 2018), www.hollywoodre porter.com/tv/tv-news/margaret-atwood-says-bulk-hulu-handmaids-tale-profits-went-mgm-1081423/.

London.[4] Due to the intense public interest in the forthcoming novel, the publishing house had even installed special anti-hacking measures to protect the unpublished manuscript.[5] No doubt, in a digital age and transmedia world, the marketing synergies between the serial adaptation and well-timed release of a sequel in novel form – and almost thirty-five years after the first installment – were also impressive.

The staggering sales numbers, however, did not destine Atwood to be a natural claimholder to the Booker, which market research by Nielsen recently confirmed as the "world's most visible literary prize."[6] She had, after all, already won the prize in 2000 with her historical novel *The Blind Assassin*.[7] In addition, with regard to literary merit, *The Testaments* was widely seen as less interesting than some of the other titles on the short list.[8] When Atwood received the prize, it was alongside a much less well-known though by no means less prolific author whose books had been produced with much smaller print runs and, above all, a smaller marketing budget and less visibility for decades: Bernardine Evaristo. The first printing of *Girl, Woman, Other* must have been small in comparison to *The Testaments*, though Evaristo had been an active and productive author for decades, too.

---

[4] Penguin Random House, "Behind the Book: Inside Vintage's Publicity Campaign for the Testaments" [blog] (December 12, 2019), www.penguin.co.uk/articles/company/blogs/behind-the-book–inside-vintage-s-campaign-for-margaret-atwood-s.html.

[5] H. Wood, "Margaret Atwood Sheds Light on Hacker's Efforts to Steal the Testaments," *The Bookseller* (September 10, 2019), www.thebookseller.com/news/margaret-atwood-discusses-attempted-cyber-theft-testaments-1079281.

[6] H. Wood, "Booker Remains World's Most Visible Literary Prize, Research Shows," *The Bookseller* (December 22, 2021), www.thebookseller.com/news/booker-remains-most-visible-literary-prize-research-shows-1296568#.

[7] Cf. M. Moseley, *A History of the Booker Prize: Contemporary Fiction since 1992* (London: Routledge, 2021), pp. 68–74.

[8] This included Lucy Ellmann's monumental, 1000-page stream-of-consciousness novel *Ducks, Newburyport*, which was published by the small independent Galley Beggar Press under significant financial risk. For further contexts, see S. Jordison, "What Happened?" *TLS* (October 25, 2019), www.the-tls.co.uk/articles/what-happened-booker-prize-ellmann/.

When *Girl, Woman, Other* was longlisted for the Booker "it did not yet have an American publisher" and the book "did not receive a review by the London *Sunday Times* until just two weeks before the ceremony."[9] Evaristo herself said that, before *Girl, Woman, Other*, she had "felt far removed from the literary mainstream and her books had yet to crack the bestseller lists."[10] Publishers also continuously contended there was "no market" for her work.[11] A changed media landscape, and shifts in the book industry regarding inclusion and (biblio)diversity may have helped pave the way for the Booker win, but the marketing campaign for Evaristo came after, not before. What happened after Evaristo's win might be called a catch-up: the bulk of her eleven books have since been republished by Penguin with new eye-catching, "instagrammable" covers.[12] Since the Booker award, accelerating the typical literary prize cascade that James F. English has observed,[13] Evaristo has received over thirty additional high-profile honors and prizes in the space of two years, which is more than she received before the Booker in her entire lifetime. The attention thus created by the Booker for Evaristo and her oeuvre – an attention bestowed on Atwood's *The Testaments* by marketing campaigns and the Netflix series before the event – underscores the significance not only of literary prizes but also of particular literary prizes, given the attention economy that is twenty-first-century publishing. Indeed, directing and redirecting considerable attention to its

---

[9] A. Russell, "How Bernardine Evaristo Conquered British Literature," *The New Yorker* (February 3, 2022), www.newyorker.com/culture/persons-of-interest/how-bernardine-evaristo-conquered-british-literature.

[10] R. Liu, "How Bernardine Evaristo Won the Booker," *Prospect*, May 2, 2020, www.prospectmagazine.co.uk/magazine/bernardine-evaristo-girl-woman-other-interview-profile.

[11] R. Liu, "How Bernardine Evaristo Won the Booker," *Prospect*, June 2020 (May 2, 2020), www.prospectmagazine.co.uk/magazine/bernardine-evaristo-girl-woman-other-interview-profile.

[12] A. Peterson, "Bernardine Evaristo's Novels Get a Makeover," *Brittle Paper* (April 13, 2020), https://brittlepaper.com/2020/04/bernardine-evaristos-novels-get-a-makeover/.

[13] See J. F. English, *The Economy of Prestige: Prizes, Awards, and the Circulation of Cultural Value* (Cambridge, MA: Harvard University Press, 2005), p. 334.

nominees and award-holders, the Booker's impact on public attention cycles is both slickly handled and enormous. It has perfected building a buzz around authors via an "elaborate selection process, which moves from a longlist (announced in July) to a shortlist (announced in September) to a gala dinner at Royal Albert Hall (in mid-October) when the winner is announced, closely accompanied by intensive media coverage, which 'generates suspense while maximizing commercial appeal'".[14]

Given the select, heavy-handed marketing of one particular text and not another, preliminary questions we might ask are: Which writers and which books are boosted in this way? As Ignacio M. Sánchez Prado reminds us, bestsellers are "manufactured," but which books are, and under whose auspices?[15] And how does the notion of books being "different" fit in with the hyper-commodification of certain "big books"[16] every season?

While the buzz-creation machine of the Booker and a select few similar literary prizes have been observed and analyzed by various scholars,[17] one

---

[14] S. Baumbach, "Marketing Anglophone World Literatures," in *Handbook of Anglophone World Literatures*, ed. S. Helgesson, B. Neumann, and G. Rippl (Berlin: De Gruyter, 2020), p. 236; see also C. Squires, "Literary Prizes and Awards," in *A Companion to Creative Writing*, ed. G. Harper (London: John Wiley, 2013), pp. 291–303, here pp. 294–297 in particular. Graham Huggan, here quoted by Baumbach, originally also discussed the Booker's colonial legacy, sitting oddly (as he argues) with its long-standing interest in postcolonial writers; indeed, Huggan refers to it "as remaining bound to an Anglocentric discourse of benevolent paternalism." See G. Huggan, "Prizing 'Otherness': A Short History of the Booker," *Studies in the Novel*, 29 (1997), 3: 412–433, p. 418, www.jstor.org/stable/29533224.

[15] I. M. Sánchez Prado, "Commodifying Mexico: On *American Dirt* and the Cultural Politics of a Manufactured Bestseller," *American Literary History*, 33 (Summer 2021), 2: 371–393, https://doi.org/10.1093/alh/ajab039.

[16] On the concept of "big books," see in detail J. B. Thompson, *Merchants of Culture: The Publishing Business in the Twenty-First Century* (London: Plume, 2012), pp. 188–222.

[17] J. F. English, *The Economy of Prestige: Prizes, Awards, and the Circulation of Cultural Value* (Cambridge, MA: Harvard University Press, 2005); C. Squires,

particular aspect about Evaristo's success that hit the headlines was the important fact that Evaristo was the first Black woman to win the prize, something that Evaristo, a longtime advocate of the voices of Black writers, built on during and after the buzz-creating Booker process. The 2019 shortlist was, in fact, the first-ever Booker shortlist without any white male authors on the list.[18] While the Booker has promoted postcolonial literatures in the past (with Salman Rushdie, Arundhati Roy, and J. M. Coetzee ranging among previous laureates),[19] Evaristo was the first female Black British author and, acutely aware of the unique position in which she found herself, she embarked on a series of awareness-raising (or attention-raising) activities especially designed to illuminate the lack of diversity in the publishing industry. Rather cynically, the need for such campaigning was underscored by none other than a BBC presenter glossing Evaristo as "another author" when describing her and Atwood's shared win of the prize. This was instantly picked up on social media including by Evaristo herself who tweeted "Pls RT: The @BBC described me yesterday as 'another author' apropos @TheBookerPrizes 2019. How quickly & casually they have removed my name from history – the first black woman to win it. This is what we've always been up against, folks."[20] The tweet garnered a sizable 9,572

Marketing Literature: The Making of Contemporary Writing in Britain (London: Palgrave Macmillan, 2007); S. Marsden, *Prizing Scottish Literature: A Cultural History of the Saltire Society Awards* (Cambridge: Cambridge University Press, 2021); M. Moseley, *A History of the Booker Prize: Contemporary Fiction since 1992* (New York: Routledge, 2022).

[18] M. Moseley, *A History of the Booker Prize: Contemporary Fiction since 1992* (New York: Routledge, 2022), p. 220.

[19] For a critical discourse on the Booker's relationship with postcolonial literature, see G. Huggan, "Prizing 'Otherness': A Short History of the Booker," *Studies in the Novel*, 29 (1997), 3: 412–433, www.jstor.org/stable/29533224.

[20] B. Evaristo (@BernardineEvari), "Pls RT: The @BBC described me yesterday as 'another author' apropos @TheBookerPrizes 2019. How quickly & casually they have removed my name from history" [Twitter post] (December 4, 2019), https://twitter.com/BernardineEvari/status/1202103687231016960; see also A. Flood, "'Another Author': Outrage after BBC Elides Bernardine Evaristo's Booker Win," *The Guardian* (December 4, 2019), www.theguardian.com/books/

Retweets, 1,100 Quote Tweets and 13.3K Likes by February 2022. As this already indicates, the attention generated in the attention economy, just like the symbolic and monetary capitals into which attention can be trans-substantiated and vice versa, are usable to diverse ends: in Evaristo's case, their energies have been aligned at least partially with diversifying efforts. And indeed, not only did Penguin start reprinting Evaristo's works in the said format alongside other novels by Black writers and/or writers of African or Asian descent, Evaristo is also using her newfound acclaim for her latest project. She is now the "curator of Black Britain: Writing Back [. . .,] a series with my publisher, Hamish Hamilton at Penguin UK, whereby we reintroduce into circulation overlooked books from the past that deserve a new readership."[21] The series has also focused on design, sporting individualized covers by handpicked illustrators and artists from diverse backgrounds.[22] Having arrived in the second decade of the twenty-first century, literature clearly can simultaneously be driven by the project of cultural participation and economic thinking – it is both culture and commodity.

While a growing chorus of scholars has pointed out different aspects of writers' entanglement in economic activities and processes,[23] in most

2019/dec/04/another-author-outrage-after-bbc-elides-bernardine-evaristo-booker-win.

[21] B. Evaristo, *Manifesto: On Never Giving Up* (London: Hamish Hamilton, 2021), p. 175; cf. C. Koegler, "Memorialising African Being and Becoming in the Atlantic World: Affective Her-Stories by Yaa Gyasi and Bernardine Evaristo," in *The Routledge Companion to Gender and Affect*, ed. T. W. Reeser (New York: Routledge, 2022), pp. 374–385.

[22] S. Carlick, "'Design Has the Power to Encourage People to Start Reading': Behind the Book Covers of Black Britain: Writing Back," *Penguin Random House* (February 5, 2021), www.penguin.co.uk/articles/2021/february/black-britain-writing-back-design-book-covers.html.

[23] The awareness of these crossovers has been particularly prominent in postcolonial studies; see for example, G. Huggan, *Postcolonial Exotic: Marketing the Margins* (London: Routledge, 2001); G. Huggan, "Re-evaluating the Postcolonial Exotic," *Interventions*, 22 (2020), 7: 808–824; S. Brouillette, *Postcolonial Writers and the Global Literary Marketplace* (London: Palgrave, 2011); S. Ponzanesi, *The*

spheres of society and in the academy, both books and literature continue to be assigned an exceptional status – a status that is fundamentally rooted in the notion of an essential *difference* of books from other market goods. This includes the legal framing, given that the "essential difference" of books has long been translated into hands-on legal regulations, whether active or passive, such as fixed book pricing or reduced VAT rates, which persist to date in many countries. The conditions in Germany (which is also the authors' current place of primary residence), can serve as a preliminary example here: books are defined in the legal texts (The German Fixed Book Price Law, "Buchpreisbindungsgesetz," established in 2002) as "cultural goods" ("Kulturgüter") on the foundation that they radically differ from "economic goods" ("Wirtschaftsgüter"), though the exact content or meaning of this difference remains opaque.[24] In 1993, with a nod toward the 1962 Restrictive Practices Court decision, Alison Baverstock asked "Are Books Different?" in her consideration of book marketing. Almost twenty years later, this Element seeks to explore the notion of books being "different" or "essential" products by focusing on two ultimately intertwined aspects: (a) the meaning of "difference" and (b) the manifold digitization processes that change how we encounter, and possibly how we perceive, literature and

Postcolonial Cultural Industry: Icons, Markets, Mythologies (London: Palgrave, 2014); J. Ramone, *Postcolonial Writers in the Local Literary Marketplace: Located Reading* (London: Palgrave, 2020); C. Koegler, *Critical Branding: Postcolonial Studies and the Market* (New York: Routledge, 2018). For a wider take, also see P. Casanova, *The World Republic of Letters* (Cambridge, MA: Harvard University Press, 2007); J. F. English, *The Economy of Prestige: Prizes, Awards, and the Circulation of Cultural Value* (Cambridge, MA: Harvard University Press, 2005); G. Sapiro, "How Do Literary Works Cross Borders (or Not)? A Sociological Approach to World Literature," *Journal of World Literature*, 1 (2016): 81–96, https://doi.org/10.1163/24056480-00101009.

[24] Cf. Deutsche Monopolkommission, "Fixed Book Prices in a Changing Market Environment," Special Report No. 80 (2018), www.monopolkommission.de/images/PDF/SG/s80_fulltext.pdf; for context and discussion, see C. A. Peter, *Kulturgut Buch: Die Legitimation des Kartellrechtlichen Preisbindungsprivilegs von Büchern – Schutzzweck, Schutzgegenstand und Wirkungen des Buchpreisbindungsgesetzes* (Berlin: Springer, 2022).

books. With a special focus on the sociopolitical, legal, economic, and cultural impacts of the notion "books are different," we seek to trouble, extend, and update "difference," our running hypothesis being that books might *not* need to be noneconomic or even anti-economic goods to prove themselves as media of particular social relevance. Instead, their potentially unique social role – fuzzy at the edges as we enter a digital age – might exactly depend on market economic mechanisms, most prominently prizes, marketing, and branding, to gain traction and unfold those socially valuable potentials that are often (if not always) also defined by a political component – such as rallying for more diversity in the publishing industry. Thus ultimately complicating current notions of "difference" in relation to "books," we suggest that books and book culture might need to be *diverse* in order to legitimately count as *different*; that is, they might need to earn the kind of protection and surplus income that strengthens publishers' and authors' structural positions via a diversification of voices both published and in gatekeeping positions. In turn, we will discuss how the rise of the digital literary sphere has been impacting the nexus of commodification and diversification.

1.1 (Biblio)diversity and the Buzz

Who gets the buzz and why? The hype surrounding and following Evaristo's Booker win could be an indicator that publishing has reached the point where diversity is getting the buzz – marketing and branding efforts, prizes, republications, cascading online waves of retweets, and attention. However, the persistence and depth of such buzz is not a foregone conclusion, nor is the problem of the lack of diversity in publishing easily resolved, and almost certainly not dispatched by Evaristo's one-off win. Also, while there has been a growing consensus in the book industry and beyond that both bibliodiversity[25] and diversity matter, it remains unclear what bibliodiversity means, how it relates to diversity issues (what kind of diversity?), and how these concepts might be translated into pragmatic structural change. For some, bibliodiversity is measured by the

---

[25] Cf. S. Hawthorne, *Bibliodiversity: A Manifesto for Independent Publishing* (North Geelong: Spinifex Press, 2014).

range of small, independent publishers in an increasingly mainstream and conglomerate-dominated market environment. In this vein, "books are different" is a notion that is lauded and upheld particularly in the sight of the "Big 5" and Amazon's growing power.[26] While small, independent presses certainly do contribute to books being available, and perhaps are able to produce "riskier" titles outside of an environment that may foster "corporate censorship,"[27] the extent to which they contribute to amplifying diverse voices and content is a wholly different matter. After all, bibliodiversity can also be understood to mean the range of titles in translation. Thus, bibliodiversity does not necessarily stand in any straightforward or measurable relation with the kind of diversity, equity, and inclusion to which the publishing industry is increasingly paying attention – albeit slowly and in patches.

Recent studies such as the Lee and Low Diversity Baseline Survey[28] and *RE:Thinking "Diversity" in Publishing*[29] have shown that publishing is overwhelmingly white and middle class. The historical depth of this problem has been given more attention in recent research, for instance by Richard Jean So with his study on the American book industry.[30] Anamik Saha and Sandra van Lente have recently positioned these issues within the cultural industries more widely and under consideration of "racial

---

[26] Cf. C. Squires, "Essential? Different? Exceptional? The Book Trade and Covid-19," *C21 Literature* [posted by K. Shaw] (December 10, 2020), https://c21 .openlibhums.org/news/403/.

[27] Cf. G. M. Schivone, "Corporate Censorship Is a Serious, and Mostly Invisible Threat to Publishing," *Electric Lit* (January 17, 2019), https://electricliterature .com/corporate-censorship-is-a-serious-and-mostly-invisible-threat-to-publish ing/.

[28] J. Alcantara, "The Diversity Baseline Survey," *Lee and Low Books* (2019), www .leeandlow.com/about-us/the-diversity-baseline-survey.

[29] Cf. A. Saha and S. van Lente, *RE:Thinking "Diversity" in Publishing* (London: Goldsmith Press, 2020), www.spreadtheword.org.uk/wp-content/uploads/ 2020/06/Rethinking_diversity_in-publishing_WEB.pdf.

[30] R. J. So, *Redlining Culture: A Data History of Racial Inequality and Postwar Fiction* (New York: Columbia University Press, 2020).

capitalism."[31] A lack of diversity is apparent in publishing's workforce as well as in its output, and these imbalances reverberate and are reinforced through the various consecratory mechanisms which cement success in the publishing industry, such as reviewing and awards. While several events of the last two years, most prominently the Black Lives Matter movement, have accelerated publishing's self-reckoning with the lack of diversity, and initial steps have been taken to counteract systemic exclusion, there is still much work to do. This is poignantly revealed by 2020's *RE:Thinking "Diversity"* study which was compiled in partnership with Goldsmiths, University of London, Spread the Word, and The Bookseller. It was foreworded by none other than Evaristo and involved 113 professionals in the publishing industry – publishing houses big and small, authors, agencies, and so forth – and focused on the lack of diversity in publishing. The industry's core target audience, the study found, continues[32] to be white and middle class, with publishing writers of color often being considered as "too commercially risky."[33] When Black authors are contracted, they and their books are frequently whitewashed or exoticized so as to appeal to the (pigeon-holing) expectations of a white audience.

These dynamics are not harnessed by Evaristo (or Abdulrazak Gurnah, to speak of the even more recent past) winning prestigious prizes, given publishing's multilayered and complex selection and curation mechanisms as well as intricate hierarchies. In fact, it might seem that literary prize committees have managed to react more quickly to criticism about the lack

---

[31] Cf. A. Saha and S. van Lente, "Diversity, Media and Racial Capitalism: A Case Study on Publishing," *Racial and Ethnic Studies*, 45 (2022), 16, 216–236. https://doi.org/10.1080/01419870.2022.2032250.

[32] As Evaristo clarifies in her foreword, *RE:Thinking "Diversity" in Publishing* builds on previous reports such as In Full Colour (Kean, 2004), Free Verse (Spread the Word, 2005), Writing the Future (Spread the Word, 2015), and Freed Verse (Teitler, 2017) which also documented that BAME authors are pressured to write stories that reproduce racial (e.g., exoticizing) stereotypes, thus not receiving the same creative freedoms as their white counterparts.

[33] A. Saha and S. van Lente, *RE:Thinking "Diversity" in Publishing* (London: Goldsmith Press, 2020), p. 10, www.spreadtheword.org.uk/wp-content/uploads/2020/06/Rethinking_diversity_in-publishing_WEB.pdf.

of diversity on judging panels and in selections than publishers have in their lists and among their employees. Given the annual nature of the prizes, the opportunity for quick renewal and diversification is (at least theoretically) higher than in publishing per se.[34] As Dan Sinykin has emphasized, "there is a long history of purported interest in diversification in publishing without follow through."[35] On the other hand, quick changes in juries might be less long-lived, and individual prize decisions do not have the power to shift systemic inequalities in a sustainable way. Anamik Saha has shown how the hyper-commercialization of the book industry over the past decades has led to rationalization processes, which in turn perpetuate the racialization of authors.[36] Saha uses the example of book covers and racist stereotypes to illustrate his point and further substantiates his argument with qualitative interviews.

As discussed by Laura McGrath, publishing's "comping" practices (i.e., comparing submitted works to already published ones to predict sales) also reinforce a white-hegemonic canon.[37] Several members of the overwhelmingly white publishing landscape are quoted in *RE:Thinking "Diversity,"* underscoring the belief that authors of color produce less valuable work. All things considered, it appears that bias, a lack of confidence regarding how to reach or create a more diverse audience, and ultimately a lack of diversity among those who make decisions (demonstrated, for example, in Lee and Low's Diversity Baseline Surveys), are primary reasons behind the imbalance. Also, it seems that those who are disenfranchised, and their views and visions, are often rejected as "lacking quality" simply when, for example,

---

[34] The NY Times notes, "Literary prizes may also make publishing appear more diverse than it actually is." R. J. So and G. Wezerek, "Just How White Is the Book Industry?" *The New York Times* (December 11, 2020), www.nytimes.com/interactive/2020/12/11/opinion/culture/diversity-publishing-industry.html.

[35] D. Sinykin, "Millennial Fiction and the Question of Generations," Paper held at MLA 2022 (2022), www.dansinykin.com/mla-2022.

[36] A. Saha, "The Rationalizing/Racializing Logic of Capital in Cultural Production," *Media Industries*, 3 (2016), 1, 1–16. https://doi.org/10.3998/mij.15031809.0003.101.

[37] L. McGrath, "Comping White," *Los Angeles Review of Books* (January 19, 2019), https://lareviewofbooks.org/article/comping-white/.

they do not centralize whiteness or refuse to cater to white assumptions of what defines the lives of people of color. Indeed, where it is considered that white readers want to read about the lives of BIPOC people, their expectations according to the report are crime stories, immigration stories, that is, stories that deal with being a BIPOC person *as* a problem or issue. This need to self-problematize/self-victimize is also familiar from publishing LGBTQIA+ literature where queerness is expected to be an issue (coming-out stories, social exclusion, depression, decline, failure, etc.[38]) which reinforces their perception as "issue-y."[39] This shows in a nutshell the extent to which (hetero-patriarchal) whiteness habitually problematizes marginal identities/positionalities rather than systemic racism, homophobia, and conscious or unconscious bias. Indeed, requiring (those perceived as) "minority" writers to write about their "issues" hampers or evades the need for actual social and political change. It is no surprise, then, that publishing largely remains a majority-white structure; that we are still in a situation where "Publishers don't have a clue about how to increase their market"[40] when thinking beyond the white-hegemonic canon and its readership. Meanwhile, underrepresentation of female writers and gatekeepers in publishing is also a long-standing issue, with studies such as the Vida Count (USA),[41] Stella Count (Australia)[42], or #Frauenzählen (Germany)

---

[38] For an apt discussion of such queer-negative perceptions, see for example L. Hess, *Queer Aging in North American Fiction* (Basingstoke: Palgrave, 2019) as well as classic works of queer theory such as J. Halberstam, *The Queer Art of Failure* (Durham: Duke University Press, 2011); E. Lee, *No Future: Queer Theory and the Death Drive* (Durham: Duke University Press, 2004).

[39] Anamik Saha used the formulation "issue-y" in a guest lecture he gave at Münster University on October 8, 2020.

[40] Cf. A. Saha and S. van Lente, *RE:Thinking "Diversity" in Publishing* (London: Goldsmith Press, 2020), p. 22, www.spreadtheword.org.uk/wp-content/uploads/2020/06/Rethinking_diversity_in-publishing_WEB.pdf.

[41] VIDA women in literary arts, www.vidaweb.org/.

[42] The Stella Count "assesses the extent of gender bias in the field of book reviewing in Australia" with the aim to: "recognise and celebrate Australian women writers' contribution to literature; bring more readers to books by

revealing the perpetual underrepresentation of women in publishing at all levels.[43]

Coming back to the question of "Are Books Still Different?" we therefore must raise the question of what "difference" could mean or should mean in current market conditions. Several decades have passed since the famous 1962 precedent at the Restrictive Practices Court of the United Kingdom, whereby fixed book prices were upheld with the reasoning that "Books are different." However, the notion that "books are different" continues to be affirmed by members of the book industry, representatives of bookshops, authors, politicians, legislators, commentators, and readers alike. The assumed "difference" of books translates into hands-on exemptions from market regulations via price fixing, Retail Price Management (RPM), discounted postage, and reduced or zero VAT rates, in some Western countries since as early as 1829.[44] Long after the demise of the

women and thus increase their sales; equip young readers with the skills to question gender disparities and challenge stereotypes; and help girls find their voice reward one writer with a $50,000 prize-money that buys a writer some measure of financial independence and thus time, that most undervalued yet necessary commodity for women, to focus on their writing" – https://thestella prize.com.au/ (January 19, 2022).

[43] "The Lack of Visibility of Female Authors in the Media. Results of a Quantitative Survey" comes to the conclusion that "Two thirds of all reviews acknowledge the works of male authors, men predominantly write about men and they get a significantly larger space provided for their reviews. Only the genre of children's and young adult literature appears to be balanced; genres such as nonfiction and crime literature that are felt to be intellectual or 'masculine' are dominated by male authors and critics." Cf. http://www.xn--frauenzhlen-r8a .de/docs/The_Lack_of_Visibility_of_Female_Authors_in_the_Media_ Results_of_a_Quantitative_Survey.pdf. Cf. very recently for the German context N. Seifert, *Frauen Literatur: Abgewertet, vergessen, wiederentdeckt* (Cologne: Kiepenheuer & Witsch, 2021).

[44] J. Poort and N. van Eijk, "Digital Fixation: The Law and Economics of a Fixed E-book Price," *International Journal of Cultural Policy*, 23 (2017), 4: 464–481, p. 464, https://doi.org/10.1080/10286632.2015.1061516.

UK Net Book Agreement in 1997, "books are different" is still the reasoning behind many state funding programs that promote national literatures and protect national book industries (e.g., Canada Book Fund, New Zealand Literary Fund, etc.).[45] If the idea that books are essential and different, and hence require special protection or promotion, continues to persist – and it does, around the world – then the question is: What kind of "difference" should be envisaged here?

1.2 Difference and Digitization

The question "Are Books Still Different?" arises with accelerated urgency in the digital age. Digitization not only affects the structural conditions of the book market and the legal status of books, but also book marketing and even how "books" themselves might be adequately understood. At times, sociopolitical debates about the book and its regulation are brought to bear on debates of national identity, and vice versa, indicating the extent to which definitions of "the book" overlap with cultural and often politicized narratives. In turn, digitization has again intensified the popular idea that both books and the book trade require protection in a changing market environment, while others are making the case that it is precisely these changes that are making some of the existing structures obsolete.

According to Joost Port and Nico van Eijk, book-related legislation in countries such as the United Kingdom, the Netherlands, and others (Germany included) "was motivated by the argument that without price fixing, retail competition would lead to fewer and less well-equipped bookshops, resulting in fewer titles published and smaller print runs, causing

---

[45] For a brief historical overview of the Net Book Agreement and its demise, please see e.g., I. Stevenson, "Distribution and Bookselling," in *The Cambridge History of the Book in Britain. Vol. 7: The Twentieth Century and Beyond*, ed. A. Nash, C. Squires, and I. Willison (Cambridge: Cambridge University Press, 2019), pp. 191–230, www.cambridge.org/core/books/cambridge-history-of-the-book-in-britain/distribution-and-bookselling/3FB119A64003691769816 D5EC4B91979#CN-bp-6.

books to become more expensive (Dearnley and Feather, 2002)."[46] As the authors suggest, the existence of physical bookstores might be seen as less urgent in a digitized market in which online retailers are increasingly contributing to ensuring that the relevant books reach customers – though it is exactly their online competition that is, of course, one of the debate's central sticking points. In Germany, these changes meant that, in 2018, the German Monopolies Commission [Deutsche Monopolkommission] suggested that parliament reevaluate the German fixed book price law ("Buchpreisbindungsgesetz," established 2002 and based on a historical precedent, much like the British Net Book Agreement). In a digitized environment, they argued, fixed book prices "slow down structural change in the brick-and-mortar book trade [. . .] and decelerate the emergence of booksellers with buyer power."[47] At the same time, they hinder the development of "efficient retailing structures" (5), "alternative sales concepts" (88), and "new customer groups."[48] Who might such "new customer groups" be?

German parliamentarians rejected the Monopolies Commission's suggestion on December 11, 2018, in a moment of singular unanimity. From the left-leaning Greens to the radical right-wing party AfD, all agreed that the advice clashed with the significant status that "the book" has commanded in German history and culture. In a joint statement, "the book" was named "Germany's bequest to world history" ["deutsches Erbe an die Weltgeschichte"],[49] going back to Johannes Gutenberg and the European

---

[46] J. Poort and N. van Eijk, "Digital Fixation: The Law and Economics of a Fixed E-book Price," *International Journal of Cultural Policy*, 23 (2017), 4: 464–481. For contexts, see also the IPA Global Fixed Book Price Report 2014: www.international publishers.org/images/news/2014/global-fixed-price-report.pdf.

[47] Deutsche Monopolkommission, "Fixed Book Prices in a Changing Market Environment," Special Report No. 80 (2018), p. 3, www.monopolkommission .de/images/PDF/SG/s80_fulltext.pdf.

[48] Deutsche Monopolkommission, "Fixed Book Prices in a Changing Market Environment," Special Report No. 80 (2018), pp. 5, 88, www.monopolkommis sion.de/images/PDF/SG/s80_fulltext.pdf.

[49] Deutscher Bundestag, "Antrag der Fraktionen der CDU/CSU und SPD 'Kulturgut Buch fördern – Buchpreisbindung erhalten'" Drucksache 19/6413 (2018), p. 1, https://dserver.bundestag.de/btd/19/064/1906413.pdf.

development of the printing press with movable type in the 1450s. Flowery terms were also used to defend the assumption that fixed book pricing and brick-and-mortar bookstores were essential precisely for maintaining a *diverse* literary landscape, but diverse in what sense? Some parliamentarians cited classic German authors such as Heinrich Heine and Hermann Hesse – two white male authors. With its nostalgic turn to the fifteenth century and its perhaps counterintuitive understanding of "diversity," the debate missed an important opportunity for considering the societal responsibilities of a book industry that is bolstered and upheld by legal protections such as, but not limited to, fixed book prices. What kind of a "diverse" literary landscape should Germany aim to have? Some of the debate's oversimplification and one-sidedness have been mirrored in the #BooksAreEssential campaign pushed during the pandemic by *Publishers Weekly*.[50] While access to books is undoubtedly important for a wide range of reasons, in a time of global crisis, likening them to items of daily necessity like food and toiletries seems problematic. It is evident that some debates surrounding books and the notion of "difference"/diversity often continue to enshrine, rather than diversify, the status quo.

And so we ask, seventy years after the Restrictive Practices Court precedent: Are Books *Still* Different? Is the value and difference attached to books timeless and untouched by societal and technological change? Are these narratives that uphold current notions of the book's essential value and difference adequate (a) in the light of the blatant lack of diversity in the publishing industry and (b) do they sufficiently reflect the changes and potential advantages that digitization is bringing – changes that indeed cater to the interests of "new" and so far often marginalized "customer groups," as suggested by the German Monopolies Commission? Burgeoning research on the "digital literary sphere"[51] is exploring the advantages of online

[50] Publishers Weekly, "Publishers Weekly Launches #BooksAreEssential – Hashtag Campaign to Support Publishing Industry in Face of Covid-19" [corporate page] (April 20, 2020), www.publishersweekly.com/pw/corp/BooksAreEssentialPressRelease.html.

[51] S. Murray, *The Digital Literary Sphere: Reading, Writing, and Selling Books in the Internet Era* (Baltimore: Johns Hopkins University Press, 2018).

spaces for literary production and discussion such as a democratization of authorship[52] and innovations in form and aesthetics, though even this sphere retains some of the caveats and pitfalls regarding equal representation and participation.[53] These discussions can be tied into observations that have been made about publics (and counterpublics) by Michael Warner, even though his work largely pre-dates the explosion of social media that the twenty-first century has seen. Warner asks, "In the media-saturated forms of life that now dominate the world, how many activities are *not* in some way oriented to publics?"[54] The digital literary sphere is a space in which publics and counterpublics are addressed and created, and in which they overlap. Publics are described by Warner as being, among other things, self-organized and constituted through attention. In an attention economy, this latter point seems particularly salient. Warner further emphasizes the way that publics are created by forming relationships among strangers, and through communication consisting of "personal and impersonal" addresses.[55]

The digital literary sphere can bring about publics as well as counter-publics. It can hold new possibilities for bibliodiversity, facilitating a more specialized catering to minority readers ranging from BIPOC to LGBTQIA+ audiences. John Keene[56] has drawn a genealogy of research on Black people's above-average participation in the digital sphere. In "The Revolution Will Be Digitized: Afrocentricity and the Digital Public Sphere," Anna Everett provides a detailed overview of Black digital counterpublics since the 1990s, which similarly undermines the myth of a

---

[52] R. L. Skains, *Digital Authorship: Publishing in the Attention Economy* (Cambridge: Cambridge University Press, 2019), www.cambridge.org/core/elements/abs/digital-authorship/C47B1D69263C882BFFC20DFD9F290F38; M. Ramdarshan Bold, "The Return of the Social Author," *Convergence: The International Journal of Research into New Media Technologie*s, 24 (2018), 2: 117–136, p. 119.

[53] A. Saha, *Race, Culture and Media* (London: Sage, Kindle ed., 2021).

[54] M. Warner, *Publics and Counterpublics* (New York: Zone Books, 2002).

[55] M. Warner, *Publics and Counterpublics* (New York: Zone Books, 2002), p. 76.

[56] J. Keene, "The Work of Black Literature in the Age of Digital Reproducibility," *Obsidian*, 41 (2015), 1/2: 288–315, p. 293, www.jstor.org/stable/44489472.

lack of Black participation in the public sphere. Catherine Knight Steele's groundbreaking work on digital Black feminism is also cautiously optimistic, pointing out the extent to which Black feminists have been using the digital literary sphere to advance Black female empowerment,[57] and Jennifer Leetsch analyses instapoetry by young Black women, underlining its potentials for self-grounding and self-representation, despite the caveats (neo-liberal marketplace; remaining hegemonies).[58] In turn, according to Caroline Duvezin, self-publishing has always been attractive to LGBTQIA+ romance authors because they could "exert more control or [. . .] curtail a lack of interest in their pitches from traditional publishers" while others take up self-publishing "partially or completely after having had bad experiences with publishers (and once they have established a loyal readership)."[59] Books that might be considered more daring or

[57] C. K. Steele, *Digital Black Feminism* (New York: New York University Press, 2021), p. 18. Steele formulates her intention thus: "Using the archival materials of Black feminist thinkers from the twentieth century (Ida B. Wells-Barnett, Zora Neale Hurston, and Anna Julia Cooper) and a curated digital collection of publicly accessible documents (tweets, and Instagram stories, and Facebook posts) from three digital Black feminist thinkers of the twenty-first century (Luvvie Ajayi, Jamilah Lemieux, and Feminista Jones), I place historical figures in Black feminist thought in conversation with digital Black feminist writers of today."

[58] J. Leetsch, "From Instagram Poetry to Autofictional Memoir and Back Again: Experimental Black Life Writing in Yrsa Daley-Ward's Work," *Tulsa Studies in Women's Literature*, 41,(2) (Fall 2022), 301–326.

[59] She further details: In the beginning particularly, digital publishing archives often proved "ephemeral." The first decade of the twenty-first century saw the rise of "a lot of new small independent e-publishers specializing in LGBTQ+ fiction and/or romance" such as Amber Quill Press "but most of the ones listed in the 'M/M (Male/Male) Romance' entry of the *Encyclopedia of Romance Fiction* have now disappeared (Markert 2018: 197), leaving behind abandoned websites or no websites at all" (C. Duvezin-Caubet, "Gaily Ever After: Neo-Victorian M/M Genre Romance for the Twenty-First Century," *Neo-Victorian Studies*, 13 [2020], 1: 246–247). Meanwhile, the dynamic nature of platforms "is not limited to small and medium independent presses" but also includes, for example, "Loveswept, Penguin Random House's digital-only imprint for romance and women's fiction"

nonmainstream by publishers are sometimes published online first and to the crowd's acclaim, before their authors are offered contracts with traditional publishers. With a focus on intersectionality, Black queer stories, too, reach wide audiences on self-publishing platforms like Wattpad. Despite these empowering and diversifying potentials, it clearly also remains important not to "make utopian pronouncements about the digital."[60] As Saha reminds us, "Western males remain the key target consumers"[61] in the bulk of online commerce and there is no guarantee that "writing is slowly becoming more open and democratic" just because "traditional publishers are no longer the sole gatekeepers of written culture."[62] And yet, digital Black feminist scholars in particular affirm the

which shut down in 2019. Yet Avon Impulse, for example, which is a "digital imprint which released most of [Cat] Sebastian's books, has been in operation since 2011 with no sign of trouble" (p. 246).

[60] A. Saha, *Race, Culture and Media* (London: Sage, Kindle ed., 2021), p. 164; see also S. C. Watkins' 2009 study *The Young and the Digital: What the Migration to Social-Network Sites, Games, and Anytime, Anywhere Media Means for Our Future* (Boston: Beacon Press, 2009); Watkins uses field interviews, surveys of college-aged students and discussions with teachers and parents to assess young people's usage of platforms such as Facebook and MySpace, and one of his observations addresses the remaining "digital divide" between different platforms that make the internet a less socially equalizing sphere than it might be, in particular with regard to class and race.

[61] A. Saha, *Race, Culture and Media* (London: Sage, Kindle ed., 2021), p. 157. As Saha also reminds his readers, "Black people in particular have been historically marginalised within and excluded by the tech industry, and this is mirrored in the very infrastructure of computing itself, where whiteness is the norm and blackness is 'the social problem' that necessitates computational solutions in order to be fixed (Benjamin, 2019; McIlwain, 2019). Indeed, many critical race scholars of technology have drawn attention to the internet as an intrinsically white space" (p. 155). For criticisms specifically regarding algorithms, see S. U. Noble, *Algorithms of Oppression: How Search Engines Reinforce Racism* (New York: New York University Press, 2018).

[62] M. Ramdarshan Bold, "The Return of the Social Author," *Convergence: The International Journal of Research into New Media Technologie*s, 24 (2018), 2: 119.

possibilities and effectiveness of online resistance (such as in relation to hashtag activism) in recent publications.[63] Indeed more tailored, including more intersectional, research might most adequately determine where (which platforms, in which forums, etc.) participation is enabled in more diversified terms or under whose auspices.

Drawing both on the continuing lack of diversity in the publishing industry and on debates surrounding digitization, especially the digital literary sphere, this Element (somewhat provocatively) inquires into whether the "difference" of books still applies and how it might be fruitfully understood today. In so doing, *Are Books Still Different?* also considers the tendency toward reticence amongst more traditional players in the book industry toward digitization. It draws attention to the flourishing online formats of reading, writing, and curation that seem to be increasingly outpacing those of more traditional institutions and, in particular, seem to shine the spotlight on forms and formats of "difference" that are instructive for debates on the inherent value of both books and literature. Do traditional cultural assumptions regarding "the book" still stand in light of the diversifying potentials of the digital literary sphere, the attention economy, and self-publishing opportunities? How does this question relate to the often-attested lack of bibliodiversity in the Anglophone book industry? Which cultural narratives of "literature," "the book," and of "difference" might be best suited to fulfill the brief of the book as an (often nationally protected) cultural "good" in the current, digitized, and globally networked conditions?

[63] R. Risam and K. B. Josephs, *The Digital Black Atlantic* (Minneapolis: University of Minnesota Press, 2021); S. J. Jackson, M. Bailey, and B. Foucault Welles, *#HashtagActivism: Networks of Race and Gender Justice* (Cambridge, MA: MIT Press, 2020); S. J. Jackson and B. Foucault Welles, "Hijacking #myNYPD: Social Media Dissent and Networked Counterpublics," *Journal of Communication*, 65 (2015), 6: 932–952; C. K. Steele, *Digital Black Feminism* (New York: New York University Press, 2021); C. K. Steele, "Black Bloggers and Their Varied Publics: The Everyday Politics of Black Discourse Online," *Television and New Media*, 19 (2018), 2: 112–127, https://doi.org/10.1177/1527476417709535.

1.3 Our Approach

To close the introduction, we will add a note on our approach. Elsewhere, we have advocated the *network* as a suitable frame through which to view books,[64] and we intend to do so here, too. Network-anchored perspectives see literature as "a network of relations" between different actors, concepts, and spheres.[65] Of course, as Ruth Ahnert et al. argue in an Element published in this same series, "Nothing is naturally a network; rather, networks are an abstraction into which we squeeze the world."[66] Alternatively, though, we might also think of "Networks [as] hav[ing] both an ontological and epistemological dimension. They are present in our material reality, for example in transportation, economic, cultural, or social configurations of exchange, but they also constitute heuristic models of understanding, visualizing, and ultimately reducing complexity."[67] If we follow the image of squeezing the literary marketplace into the abstraction of a network this proves fruitful yet also reveals some ontological truths. In our understanding, literature requires a perspective that "combines aspects and caters to understandings of value that are commonly disciplinarily disentangled from one another"; this means connecting literature's realm of ideas and ideals with the commercial side, which is a side that "is habitually disavowed particularly in literary studies, even where literature is readily perceived as a powerful means of

---

[64] Lanzendörfer, T., and Norrick-Rühl, C, *The Novel as Network: Forms, Ideas, Commodities* (London: Palgrave Macmillan, 2020); C. Koegler, "Uneasy Forms of Interdisciplinarity: Literature, Business Studies, and the Limits of Critique," *Anglistik: International Journal of English Studies*, 32 (2021), 3: 33–51, https://doi.org/10.33675/ANGL/2021/3/6.

[65] Lanzendörfer, T., and Norrick-Rühl, C, *The Novel as Network: Forms, Ideas, Commodities* (London: Palgrave Macmillan, 2020), pp. 1–3.

[66] R. Ahnert, S. E. Ahnert, C. N. Coleman, and S. B. Weingart, *The Network Turn: Changing Perspectives in the Humanities* (Cambridge: Cambridge University Press, 2020), https://doi.org/10.1017/9781108866804.

[67] See R. Schober, "Adaptation as Connection: A Network Theoretical Approach to Convergence, Participation, and Co-production," in *Adaptation in the Age of Media Convergence*, ed. J. Fehrle and W. Schäfke (Amsterdam: Amsterdam University Press, 2019), pp. 31–56, 44.

public participation."[68] Somewhat mirroring differentiations such as "cultural good" vs. "economic good" (or literature as culture vs. commodities), the bulk of literary and cultural scholars dismiss literature's own entanglements with commerce (literature *as* commodity), or even treat it "as diametrically opposed to [literature's] progressive impacts and goals."[69] This occurs in a Bourdieusian fashion whereby symbolic capital in the literary field is supposedly generated by disavowing literature's ties to the economic. The network approach that we also utilize in this Element reestablishes these ties seeking to overcome the "cognitive dissonance"[70] caused by literature's simultaneous existence as culture and commodity, arguing that this integration does not jeopardize literature's potential for ethicality or special social status. Indeed, acknowledging literature's affinity to the (performative) market,[71] and increasingly also to digitization, unlocks new potentials both for literary practice and debates on literature's "singularity." In discussing this from an interdisciplinary perspective (book studies and literary studies), and as academics based in Germany with close academic and biographical ties to the Anglophone world, we aim for a perspective on the question of "Are Books Still Different?" that is comparative, and also itself draws on a variety of arguments that represent (what we understand as) the "network" character of the book and of our own inquiry.

Our Element will first discuss issues of "difference" as discourse, policy, and brand/ing (Section 2), followed by a more detailed analysis of what "difference" means in an increasingly digital age (Section 3). Finally, in a

[68] C. Koegler, "Uneasy Forms of Interdisciplinarity: Literature, Business Studies, and the Limits of Critique," *Anglistik: International Journal of English Studies*, 32 (2021), 3: 36, https://doi.org/10.33675/ANGL/2021/3/6.

[69] C. Koegler, "Uneasy Forms of Interdisciplinarity: Literature, Business Studies, and the Limits of Critique," *Anglistik: International Journal of English Studies*, 32 (2021), 3: 36, https://doi.org/10.33675/ANGL/2021/3/6.

[70] C. Koegler, "Uneasy Forms of Interdisciplinarity: Literature, Business Studies, and the Limits of Critique," *Anglistik: International Journal of English Studies*, 32 (2021), 3: 36, https://doi.org/10.33675/ANGL/2021/3/6.

[71] C. Koegler, *Critical Branding: Postcolonial Studies and the Market* (London: Routledge, 2018).

case study linked to this introduction, we will consider the role of Bernardine Evaristo's Booker Prize win and her place within a networked literary marketplace (Section 4). Our conclusion may not answer the question whether books are still different, but will come back to issues raised here: Who defines "the book"? Are books neutral? Who defines "difference"? And even: Whose privileges are protected through narratives of essential literary difference? Finally, the conclusion will seek to invite debate surrounding the role of literature as culture and commodity in society today.

2 What's the "Difference"? "Difference" as Discourse, Policy, and Brand/ing

In 1993, considering Australian book policies and the global trend toward multimedia conglomeration, John Curtain observed that the book is seen as superior to other media and revered as a "sacred icon."[72] Elsewhere, he argued similarly, stating that "the book sector is the enigma among media industries. Lacking the personalities and politics of television, radio and newspapers, the book is often neglected in any comparative review of contemporary media; yet the book, as a cultural icon, commands a prestige in society which is unique."[73] This mystification of the book, which can evoke associations with Walter Benjamin's ideas of the "aura" of the book, coalesces in the argument that "books are different." Curtain's perceptive description still rings true, even thirty years later; as Ted Striphas notes in *The Late Age of Print* (2009), "The notion that books belong at a significant remove from the realm of economic necessity is one of the most entrenched myths of contemporary book culture."[74] Tellingly, in central texts about the industry, John B. Thompson has termed booksellers and publishers as "merchants of culture," and Laura J. Miller has offered the image of "reluctant capitalists" for booksellers.[75] While it might seem that the book has seen its illustrious position partially eroded with the fall of the UK's Net Book Agreement in 1997 or Switzerland's fixed book price in 2011, supermarket sales, and the often-lamented rise of rival media (most recently, streaming media) or Amazon, it remains a fact that there are still

---

[72] J. Curtain, "Takeovers, Entertainment, Information & the Book," *Media Information Australia*, 68 (1993), 1: 43–48, p. 43, https://doi.org/10.1177/1329878X9306800108.

[73] Qtd in A. Baverstock, "Marketing for Publishing," in *Oxford Handbook of Publishing*, ed. A. Phillips and M. Bhaskar (Oxford: Oxford University Press, 2019), p. 4/22, online version.

[74] T. Striphas, *The Late Age of Print: Everyday Book Culture from Consumerism to Control* (New York: Columbia University Press, 2009), p. 6.

[75] J. B. Thompson, *Merchants of Culture: The Publishing Business in the Twenty-First Century* (London: Plume, 2012); L. J. Miller, *Reluctant Capitalists: Bookselling and the Culture of Consumption* (Chicago: University of Chicago Press, 2006).

countless ways in which books are protected through cultural policies and legal frameworks. Examples include lower postage for printed wares, lower VAT rates (or even zero VAT rates) for certain publications, government subsidies for books, translations, and publishers, or, in some Scandinavian markets, guaranteed print runs that are purchased by the government and distributed to public libraries.[76]

This section, then, will entangle the various forms in which the "difference" of books becomes apparent, starting with a brief analysis of "difference" as discourse, followed by observations on the implementation of "difference" in cultural policies, and then by considering "difference" as a performative branding strategy.

2.1 *"Difference" as Discourse*

In the debates surrounding the "difference" of books, it seems to be unclear wherein exactly the difference lies. Often, books are compared with other commodities such as oranges, soap, or shoes, and "difference" is encoded by claiming that books are a different type of commodity. This discourse has a long history. As Julia Bangert has shown, the discourse of "difference" was already applied in the early modern period, when the "difference" of the book as a special commodity was also connected to an alleged higher social status of booksellers. For instance, in early modern texts, booksellers were described as being more honest and laudable than other salespeople.[77] This transhistorical discourse, as affective rhetoric,[78] continues to the

---

[76] For context, cf. E. Böker, *Skandinavische Bestseller auf dem deutschen Buchmarkt: Analyse des gegenwärtigen Literaturbooms* (Würzburg: Königshausen & Neumann, 2018), pp. 50–64, especially 61–62.

[77] For details, see J. Bangert, *Buchhandelssystem und Wissensraum in der frühen Neuzeit* (Berlin: De Gruyter Saur, 2019), pp. 281–306, https://doi.org/10.1515/9783110616521.

[78] On affective rhetoric in policymaking, cf. T. Lähdesmäki, A. K. Koistinen, and S. C. Ylönen, "Affective Rhetoric and 'Sticky Concepts' in European Education Policy Documents," in *Intercultural Dialogue in the European Education Policies* (Cham: Palgrave Macmillan, 2020), pp. 81–98. https://doi.org/10.1007/978-3-030-41517-4_5.

present day with the oft-repeated "books are different." Across the board, people and even whole industries exhibit what might best be termed an affective investment in the "difference" of the book vis-à-vis other types of commodities. To avoid repeating these well-documented tropes here, it is perhaps more fruitful to look at the current situation, over eighteen months into a pandemic that has swept the globe, changed markets and priorities, and also left a palpable, though not yet measurable, impact on the book industry.

Despite the importance of screens and screen-based activities from homeschooling to socially distanced get-togethers during the pandemic, early evidence suggests that books have made a comeback over the past months. This applies to books as digital products as well as the more traditional hard-copy formats. Indeed, listening to audiobooks and podcasts – formats that allow for mobility while reading – saw a surge in popularity during the many state-instigated lockdowns. In conditions very much defined by indoor confinement, these book forms can be enjoyed while walking or otherwise exercising which, at several points in the 2020 and 2021 lockdowns, became a condition in several countries for being allowed outdoors.[79] Rereading the classics became fashionable. Accommodating the renewed interest in book products, in some locations and phases of the pandemic, bookstores were allowed to remain open during the shutdowns, underlining their product's special status. Of course, offering curbside pickup does not replace browsing as an experience and, more importantly, precludes the social functions that bookstores can fulfill.[80] While book-stores, as one of the most public spaces for book visibility and literary

---

[79] M. Sweney, "Pandemic Drives Ebook and Audiobook Sales by UK Publishers to All-Time High," *The Guardian* (November 14, 2020), www.theguardian.com/books/2020/nov/14/pandemic-drives-ebook-and-audiobook-sales-by-uk-pub lishers-to-all-time-high-covid; E. Nawotka, "European E-book, Audiobook Sales See Pandemic Pop," *Publishers Weekly* (August 13, 2020), www.publish ersweekly.com/pw/by-topic/international/international-book-news/article/ 84080-european-e-book-audiobook-sales-see-pandemic-pop.html.

[80] For contexts, cf. K. Kinder, *The Radical Bookstore: Counterspace for Social Movements* (Minneapolis: University of Minnesota Press, 2021).

communication,[81] were often forced to shift to new forms of marketing and communication,[82] access to books was framed as "essential" by trade organizations and booksellers themselves, for example, through the #BooksAreEssential hashtag launched by *Publishers Weekly* in April 2020. Similarly, in France, the "publishers' association, the Syndicat national de l'édition (SNE), joined with its booksellers' association, the Syndicat de la Librairie Française (SLF), and authors' group, the Conseil Permanent des Ecrivains (CPE), in a call for bookshops to remain open alongside supermarkets and pharmacies."[83] Interestingly, in the middle-term, the pandemic also led to new bookstores opening, as rents decreased, as reported by *Publishers Weekly* in late 2021.[84]

The pandemic developments and resulting framings reprise the question of whether books should be treated as "different" than other commodities. But it is interesting, perhaps, that libraries, which were also closed and are arguably more accessible, more equalizing, and more democratic spaces than bookstores, were often excluded from the "books are essential" campaigns. In fact, library closures and the detrimental effect of a lack of book accessibility for families, or for readers who cannot buy books but

---

[81] Cf. A. Steiner, "Select, Display, and Sell: Curation Practices in the Bookshop," *Logos*, 28 (2017), 4: 18–31, https://doi.org/10.1163/1878-4712-11112138.

[82] K. Mactavish, "Crisis Book Browsing: Restructuring the Retail Shelf Life of Books," in *Bookshelves in the Age of the COVID-19 Pandemic*, ed. C. Norrick-Rühl and S. Towheed (London: Palgrave, 2022), pp. 49–68.

[83] A. Flood, "French Bookshops Ask to Be Treated as Essential Services during new Lockdown," *The Guardian* (October 29, 2020), www.theguardian.com/books/2020/oct/29/french-bookshops-ask-to-be-treated-as-essential-services-during-new-lockdown; see also, inter alia, A. Flood, "England's Bookshops Should Be Classed as Essential, Booksellers Argue," *The Guardian* (November 10, 2020), https://amp.theguardian.com/books/2020/nov/10/englands-book shops-should-be-classed-as-essential-booksellers-argue?__twitter_impression= true.

[84] See J. Rosen, "Another Pandemic Surprise: A Mini Indie Bookstore Boom," *Publishers Weekly* (October 15, 2021), www.publishersweekly.com/pw/by-topic/industry-news/bookselling/article/87648-another-pandemic-surprise-a-mini-indie-bookstore-boom.html.

would very much like to read them, have received little attention.[85] It might seem that their remaining open would have done little for the publishing industry's revenues, or even undermined the surge in book sales, and thus they were not included in the general attention raised by the industry for the importance of book availability. Libraries were not looped into these discussions either, and it is not the first time that the significance of libraries has either been overlooked or overtly viewed in hostile ways by the trade. In the late nineteenth century, "there was a general perception that the book trade was in crisis" due to the soaring popularity of circulating and traveling libraries.[86] Reminiscent of framings of digitization as a threat both to the book trade and the book, traveling libraries were perceived to unhinge the workings of the book market, not least because they decreased publisher agency over who could access books and at what cost. As such, while the possibility of filling "pandemic bookshelves" was widely projected as essential – as a lifeline and human right – gatekeeping mechanisms were nonetheless in operation, mechanisms that tailored both "essence" and "access" according to some interests on the supply-side and not others.[87]

---

[85] For observations on book accessibility in the pandemic, cf. e.g., L. Guernsey, S. Prescott, and C. Park, "Public Libraries and the Pandemic," *New America* (2021), https://files.eric.ed.gov/fulltext/ED612400.pdf. Cf. also, more broadly, C. Norrick-Rühl, "Elmer the Elephant in the Zoom Room? Reflections on Parenting, Book Accessibility and Screen Time in a Pandemic," in *Bookshelves in the Age of the COVID-19 Pandemic*, ed. C. Norrick-Rühl and S. Towheed (London: Palgrave, 2022), pp. 195–214.

[86] I. Stevenson, "Distribution and Bookselling," in *The Cambridge History of the Book in Britain. Vol. 7: The Twentieth Century and Beyond*, ed. A. Nash, C. Squires, and I. Willison (Cambridge: Cambridge University Press, 2019), pp. 191–230, www.cambridge.org/core/books/cambridge-history-of-the-book-in-britain/distribution-and-bookselling/3FB119A64003691769816D5EC4B91979#CN-bp-6. Cf. also, in more detail, I. Stevenson, *Book Makers: British Publishing in the Twentieth Century* (London: The British Library Publishing Division, 2010), pp. 1–29.

[87] Cf. C. Norrick-Rühl and S. Towheed, "Introduction," in *Bookshelves in the Age of the COVID-19 Pandemic*, ed. C. Norrick-Rühl and S. Towheed (London: Palgrave, 2022), pp. 1–27.

As a not entirely unrelated caveat, it still remains to be seen how the uneven, gendered dynamics of care and work in the home office will impact book-shelves later on in the (ongoing) pandemic or post-pandemic times. As multiple studies have shown, numbers of submissions by women academics dropped sharply while submissions by men remained relatively stable.[88] It is entirely possible that this pattern will also have an effect on the existing gender imbalance in the fiction and nonfiction sectors as well.

While the social status of books and literature has thrived during the pandemic and in many social contexts, the tropes surrounding the idea that "books are different" have been legion, and permeated national boundaries, cultures, and languages, for a much longer time. As touched upon above, unsurprisingly, books are not oranges, soap, or shoes – and sources under-lining this difference date back to at least the seventeenth century. This includes narratives that booksellers are not "regular" salespeople. One prominent example is the depiction of bookselling as a profession by Tommaso Garzoni in his pan-European bestseller, *La Piazza Universale di tutti die professioni del mondo* (transl. "The Universal marketplace of all the professions in the world"; first Italian edition 1585, translated into Latin, German and Spanish). As several book historians have discussed, this detailed description of booksellers and their role already emphasizes the special status of selling books versus other commodities.[89]

The perceived need to distinguish the book from the market/the economic (an idea that goes back to the Romantic age[90]) remains an intriguing aspect of the question "Are Books Still Different?" It certainly also remains one of the most prominent *discursive* pillars of state-owned,

---

[88] Cf. for instance A. K. Ribarovska, M. R. Hutchinson, Q. J. Pittman, C. Pariante, and S. J. Spencer, "Gender Inequality in Publishing during the COVID-19 Pandemic," *Brain Behavior, and Immunity*, 91 (2021): 1–3, https://doi.org/10.1016/j.bbi.2020.11.022.

[89] Most recently discussed by J. Bangert, *Buchhandelssystem und Wissensraum in der frühen Neuzeit* (Berlin: De Gruyter Saur, 2019), pp. 301–305, www.degruyter.com/document/doi/10.1515/9783110616521/html.

[90] S. Brouillette, *Literature and the Creative Economy* (Redwood City: Stanford University Press, 2014).

book-promoting measures, as has also been noted by other critics. We have already mentioned Ted Striphas in this regard. For Claire Squires, "given that other products which are also untaxed or taxed at a lower rate include children's clothes, most food and fuel, the 'difference' cannot be solely one of *cultural* value."[91] The lack of certainty in defining "value," "difference," even "books" and their "diversity" in relation to books, creates a multi-directional network of meanings and references that is suitably mirrored by, and indeed might require, an interdisciplinary approach: while governments and book industries need hands-on regulations that define how book products enter the market – and this is the perspective also taken by book studies – from a literary studies perspective, some of the legal criteria do not come close to grasping what is special about *literature*, signaling that the evocative nature of "the book" changes depending on who looks at it. Because of these necessary changes in perspective and the necessarily divergent outcomes, the *difference* of books not only remains a cornerstone of book policy in different parts of the world, but is also a discourse, rather than an unambiguous fact. As a discourse, it intertwines a plurality of meanings of "difference." These meanings include, but are not limited to: narratives, even myths, as well as perspectives of power and privilege (contested, constantly renegotiated, defended).

Scaling up the idea that "books are different," Philipps and Bhaskar provide the poignant notion that "Publishing is different,"[92] explaining that "The interplay of history and modernity, tradition and innovation; the excitement of working at the frontiers of thought and culture; the ongoing ability to, just maybe, help change the world: this is why publishing is different."[93] This discourse, then, defines the notion that "difference" needs to be reflected in policy (see Section 2.2). For Bhaskar and Phillips, this is most certainly the case, as they connect the well-being of the publishing

[91] C. Squires, *Marketing Literature: The Making of Contemporary Writing in Britain* (London: Palgrave Macmillan, 2007), p. 47, emphasis CS.

[92] A. Phillips and M. Bhaskar, "Introduction," in A. Phillips and M. Bhaskar, eds., *Oxford Handbook of Publishing* (Oxford: Oxford University Press, 2019), p. 16.

[93] A. Phillips and M. Bhaskar, "Introduction," in A. Phillips and M. Bhaskar, eds., *Oxford Handbook of Publishing* (Oxford: Oxford University Press, 2019), p. 3.

industry to the well-being of society: "Publishing is one of the crucial conduits via which information, knowledge, and culture are disseminated; and in so doing it has an integral role in regulating how we live, what we believe, what we can know, when and how, what stories define us. [. . .] Without publishing, a society is, as a collective, essentially voiceless."[94] This passionate description of publishing raises questions: Which stories define us? Who is "us" if we consider the average book-buyer or the average reader? What about people who cannot read, or choose not to read for pleasure, perhaps because they feel ill-represented by what is on offer in the average bookstore? Can publishing really reflect society? Clearly, "the publishing industry" is not a neutral operatus and the kinds of knowledge promoted rather depend on the actors and gatekeepers involved. Also, icons of culture or not, books can transport constructive just as much as destructive, even toxic knowledge(s) that are ultimately not in the interest of people's, or some people's, well-being.

In sum, while we are not arguing that specific *contents* should be promoted or protected, we are suggesting that setting incentives to increase diversity might be productive in rethinking and updating "difference" as a concept. After all, if books are "different" or publishing is "different," then in what sense are they different or should they be different? How does "difference" relate to "diversity"? What is the target of the notion of diversity – is it only the outlets or a range in titles, or is there a need to accept the argument that Evaristo and others have been making: that the people who curate and write must be diverse, too, as otherwise published works are only an echo-chamber? While "books are different" remains a wide-spread and intuitively sensical assertion, why exactly this is so and, particularly, what kinds of difference we are talking about or should be talking about, remains shrouded in mystery.

2.2 *"Difference" as Policy*

Notwithstanding the insecurities surrounding "difference" as discourse, book industries have fashioned their own agreements and policymakers

---

[94] A. Phillips and M. Bhaskar, "Introduction," in A. Phillips and M. Bhaskar, eds., *Oxford Handbook of Publishing* (Oxford: Oxford University Press, 2019), pp. 7–8.

have enacted policies, principles, and even laws that protect the special status of the book. These policies have recently received more attention in the field of book studies. In her book *European Book Cultures. Diversity as a Challenge*, Stephanie Kurschus compared and contrasted European book industries and their multifarious ways to support publishing in a heterogeneous European market that earlier in this decade included global players like France, the United Kingdom, and Germany alongside tiny markets from countries with no long publishing tradition, struggling with the challenges of publishing in a language that is only accessible to a limited number of readers.[95] Her literature review offers insights into the complexities of nation-states within Europe enacting diverse cultural policies which influence publishing, bookselling, and book culture more widely. Most of the data Kurschus analyzes is well over ten years old (2007 is the year chosen as the sample), but the methodology and challenges she identifies are still relevant for understanding book policy today.

When looking at and comparing forms of book policy and book promotion, Kurschus states, the "objectives of cultural politics have been criticized as being vague; the countries do not specify their intentions when intervening in the market in favor of cultural goods such as books."[96] This is a critical point: in German debates, for instance, the fixed book price law has been criticized for its vagueness and for its preconceived but not elucidated notions of "book culture." Nonetheless, widespread "European cultural policy expresses a need" – or a desire? – "for a more diversified book sector than a free market can provide" – or is thought to be able to provide.[97] This implicit criticism of the free market goes beyond what this Element is trying to discuss, but the juxtaposition of "culture" and "market" as a rationale for book policy seems key here.

[95] S. Kurschus, *European Book Cultures: Diversity as a Challenge* (Wiesbaden: Springer VS, 2014).

[96] S. Kurschus, *European Book Cultures: Diversity as a Challenge* (Wiesbaden: Springer VS, 2014), p. 231.

[97] S. Kurschus, *European Book Cultures: Diversity as a Challenge* (Wiesbaden: Springer VS, 2014), pp. 240–241.

In general, when considering book policy measures, we can differentiate between measures that apply to all books and are extended to other forms of printed matter, and other measures which are more specifically targeted toward certain areas of the market (e.g., the trade sector), genres or groups of readers (e.g., children's book publishers), or language promotion (e.g., grants for titles in a certain language, or for translations from a certain language). As Kurschus discusses, there is also a disconnect between support systems and policies for the production of more bibliodiversity – and the consumption of those titles by readers. A recent study by Luise Hertwig has tried to tease apart the differences between the bibliodiversity produced by publishers and the bibliodiversity consumed by readers, with a focus on the French book market. Her excellent study exhibits the challenges of measuring different forms of bibliodiversity and their production and consumption.[98]

Looking further afield, Peter Read conducted a comparative study of government support for books in Canada, France, Germany, and the United Kingdom, published a few years ago in 2015.[99] His descriptive study focused on a plethora of measures and policies implemented in the four different national contexts. He structured them according to what he calls direct and indirect support for publishing. Measures he analyzed include, but are not limited to, fixed book prices, sales tax reductions, and reduced postal rates alongside other legal frameworks. In Canada, for instance, this includes the Canada Investment Act which is meant to protect Canadian publishing companies (and other media companies) from foreign control. Given the location and history of Canada, as well as its production of books in English and French – thus placing Canadian publishers either in

---

[98] L. Hertwig, *Bibliodiversität im Kontext des französischen Ehrengastauftritts Francfort en français auf der Frankfurter Buchmesse 2017: Die ganze Vielfalt des Publizierens in französischer Sprache?* Unpublished PhD dissertation, University of Flensburg (2022).

[99] P. F. Read, *On Culture and Commerce: A Comparison of Government Support for Book Publishing in Canada, France, Germany and the United Kingdom*, Inaugural dissertation (2015) https://openscience.ub.uni-mainz.de/bitstream/20.500.12030/4045/1/100000508.pdf.

direct competition with the US and UK markets and/or the French market –
the question in Canada is not so much whether books are different, but rather
how to maintain and support the "difference" of Canadian books, written and
published in Canada.

This indicates the nationalistic dimension of protecting "book culture."
Indeed, Poort and van Eijk discuss a whole range of national incarnations of
dealing with the "difference" of literature:

> Slovenia, for instance, introduced a fixed book price law
> only in 2014, Israel in 2013, while in Poland, the Polish
> Chamber of Books has drafted a bill only recently and is
> currently lobbying to have it adopted. Quebec (Canada),
> Hungary and Denmark have recently had discussions on
> whether a fixed price for books should be (re)introduced
> (IPA 2014). Meanwhile, other countries have repealed exist-
> ing price fixing agreements, often prompted by competition
> policy: Sweden, Finland and Australia in the 1970s, the UK
> and Ireland in 1995, Switzerland in 1999 and Hungary in
> 2007 (OECD 2012, IPA 2014). Ten of the countries with a
> fixed book price [. . .] are EU members, despite RPM being a
> hard-core   restriction   under   the   Block   Exemption
> Regulation. The European Commission does not favour
> fixed book price laws, but accepts them as long as they do
> not hinder cross-border trade between member states
> (European Commission 2002).[100]

In its widely received Fixed Book Price Report in 2014 (to date the
only edition of the report), the International Publishers Association
(IPA) asserted that it does not advocate for or against fixed book

---

[100] J. Poort and N. van Eijk, "Digital Fixation: The Law and Economics of a Fixed
E-book Price," *International Journal of Cultural Policy*, 23 (2017), 4: 464–481,
p. 468, https://pure.uva.nl/ws/files/19091793/2017_Poort_van_Eijk_Digital_
fixation_the_law_and_economics_of_a_fixed_e_book_price.pdf.

prices.[101] Undeniably, though, its members (national publishers associations from across the globe), do take a stance in these debates.

While the fixed book price debate is more messy and entangled in national book trade and publishing histories – for example, in the USA, any attempts at price fixing were obliterated with the Supreme Court decision of 1914 – the tax rate on books is an easier issue to advocate for. In this case, the IPA has clearly taken a stance and called upon all nations to zero-rate the VAT on books:

> A zero rate of VAT on all titles boosts consumption of literature generally and of textbooks in the classroom and at home. Books deliver knowledge, but the book market is highly price-sensitive. Any increase in cost, however small, can inflict serious damage to sales and therefore future investment in more innovative and effective titles. In order to support the knowledge economy, to encourage reading and to promote the benefits of lifelong education, the IPA recommends zero-rate VAT for all books, no matter what their format or how they are accessed.[102]

As previously discussed, there are numerous additional forms of policy-making which can protect books as well, and these are often nationally motivated. A peculiar – and oft-debated – example is that of Australia's Parallel Importation Restrictions (PIRs) which underscores the significance of territorial copyright. The PIRs give Australian-based publishers a window of opportunity to publish and sell US and UK bestsellers within their own imprints, and thus a chance to profit from "big books," as Thompson

---

[101] Cf. International Publishers Association, "Global Fixed Book Price Report" (May 23, 2014), p. 1, www.internationalpublishers.org/images/news/2014/global-fixed-price-report.pdf.

[102] International Publishers Association and Federation of European Publishers, "VAT on Books: The IPA-FEP Annual Global Report 2018" (2018), p. 4, https://internationalpublishers.org/images/aa-content/news/news-2019/IPA_ANNUAL_GLOBAL_REPORT_2018_2.pdf.

terms them, which help subsidize other projects in-house. As the Australian Society of Authors indicates, the benefits for the national market – and Australian authors – are manifold.[103]

Indirect support for publishing, authors, and books can also come through funding schemes that target independent publishers and financially risky or untenable publishing projects. Examples of institutions in the anglophone world that fund or have funded publishing activities are the Arts Councils in England, Ireland, Scotland, and Wales; the Canada Book Fund; the Australian Council of Arts; or the Arts Council of New Zealand. In post-devolution and postcolonial contexts, these organizations pay special heed to funding projects incorporating small languages or indigenous voices, sometimes offering extra funding or incentives to diversify book production.

All these policies and measures – whether they support publishing, books, and authors directly or indirectly – find their reasoning in the discourse of "difference." Whether or not these measures work and make sense is a different issue that we cannot treat in any depth here: such measures as national book funds in some countries, VAT cuts in others, or setting book prices and introducing minimum book prices either on the basis of agreements between booksellers and the book industry or through legislation, such as in Germany; with effects including promoting national authors, stimulating cross-subsidization, enhancing bibliodiversity, keeping intact the availability of books through the brick-and-mortar trade, maintaining print runs, and promoting national literatures, particularly where a lack of language barriers (as in the anglophone book market) would mean that competition from outside would outperform the sale of national book products. The measures lead us to wonder: When books are poised to enter the market as protected goods, how are they branded and sold?

2.3 *"Difference" as (Performative) Branding*

If difference is both discourse and policy, then an important aspect of this is that discourse is also, always, a symbolic economy. In the symbolic

---

[103] Australian Society of Authors, Campaign: Parallel Importation, www .asauthors.org/campaigns/parallel-importation.

economy of discourse, "any influential idea, position, and positionality; form of resistance or mainstream; and any academic field or socioeconomic and cultural formation, in order to gain prominence, will depend on successful narratives and embodiments through which it will be valorised."[104] It is a context where "successful narratives and embodiments" point us to the extent to which both social change and attempts at maintaining the status quo rely on brand acts.[105] Brand acts see individuals and collectives try to intervene in ways that come to *attention* – to interlink both notions of economy: the attention economy and the symbolic economy of discourse. This does not mean that people who engage in performative branding (we all do; this Element does) or respond to performative branding are either profit-oriented or duped by the logics of commodification. Instead, it means that people do not relate randomly or without prompting to specific ideas, arguments, narratives, persons, and so on, but do so on the grounds of what they perceive as (in whatever form) valorizable in the widest sense (useful, urgent, touching, pragmatically necessary, etc.) in given conditions.

As this already suggests, discourse does not contain neutral terms, that is, terms that are not in some way valorized or valorizable, wittingly or unwittingly. "Book" and "literature" are pertinent examples, and so is "Books are different." "Book" is not a neutral term or concept, and it particularly is not where we emphasize its (or literature's) inherent cultural value or worthiness of protection. Indeed, the socially widespread assumption that the book is a "cultural good" can be understood as the result of a mass accumulation of brand acts that have rendered salient and valuable a certain understanding of "book" – in the interest of certain players, of course, whoever they may be (potentially society as a whole).

What is more, it is important to pay heed to the affective components of performative branding: not only is performative branding infused with human energy and time, but also with a whole variety of positive and, at

---

[104] C. Koegler, *Critical Branding: Postcolonial Studies and the Market* (New York: Routledge, 2018), p. 3.

[105] C. Koegler, *Critical Branding: Postcolonial Studies and the Market* (New York: Routledge, 2018), p. 3.

times, negative emotions, ranging from enthusiastic passion and altruism to dread or malice or narcissistic pleasure. Indeed, in the symbolic economy of *literary* discourse, there are always some authors/narratives/voices that are considered more valorizable than others and some are not deemed valorizable at all. Historically, of course, the criteria for valorization shift or are extended, for which the rise of feminist literary studies, the rediscovery of prominent eighteenth-century novelists, or indeed the push for more diversity in literature and the publishing industry are poignant examples. Value; that which is considered valorizable; that which *is* successfully valorized (because some ideas rise to the top more easily than others) is always curated, and is done so in the interest of some people and not others. Trying to break through the layers and walls shored up by conventional branding and symbolic economies of scale (meaning you can leverage an already-strong position) can be difficult or take disproportionate amounts of energy. Brand narratives can be solidly in place and naturalized to the extent that the labor it has taken to normalize them all but disappears from attention. Striphas similarly observes "the degree to which certain economic realities of the book trade have come to be seen as so customary, so banal, as to be overlooked almost entirely today."[106] Indeed, heightened attention to these realities can be unwelcome from the point of view of those in whose interest such normalization operates. (A Marxist argument could be strung from this, but we will leave this for another publication.)

What does all this mean, then, for "books are different," other than that this statement represents an almost paradigmatic example of performative branding in a performative market[107] – a market that underlies public debate as much as it does academia? It means that, specifically, the distinction of "cultural good" vs. "economic good"; the understanding that books are, somehow, at a remove from "the market" or essentially anti-market, may be a naturalized and valorized notion, but not necessarily grounded in the ways in which books are, in fact, brought to the market and become

---

[106] T. Striphas, *The Late Age of Print: Everyday Book Culture from Consumerism to Control* (New York: Columbia University Press, 2009), p. 6.

[107] Cf. C. Koegler, *Critical Branding: Postcolonial Studies and the Market* (New York: Routledge, 2018).

visible as market products. After all, books are products that are produced, marketed, and sold in actual markets. They are valorized or devalorized – the amount of gatekeeping that goes into the process of having specific books come to attention in society, from literary agents to reviewers to prize-awarding committees, should dispel any easy thinking that books stand outside the logics of capital accumulation (be that accumulation of social, cultural, or monetary capital) or that their relationship to these logics can be grasped in binary terms (such as commodification vs. artistic autonomy[108]). The content of books – some might call it literature – is just as entangled in these kinds of accumulating processes: narratives contain appeals for readers to follow particular patterns of valorization or de-valorization. They contain brand acts and interact with social brand narratives (either subtly or unsubtly, wittingly or unwittingly) whereby they seek to hook readers and win them over to certain ideas, or positions, or instill awe in them for their aesthetic properties. And even books that were never intended to be read by anyone might, when discovered hundreds of years later in an archive, trigger a whole plethora of brand acts, positive or negative, when pertinently chiming with a reader's and their culture's normative conventions of valuation.

Both literature and books, then, are conceptual sites of instrumentalization, politicization, valorization, and consolidation, given that it is in the symbolic economy of discourse that they can, potentially, become salient and garner attention. In turn, whatever is successfully branded as "literature" or "book" will be viewed and treated differently, perhaps favorably, yielding symbolic, cultural, and monetary capital for authors and/or publishers, or readers who are spotted giving attention to something so valuable. These processes are potentially diversified and democratized[109] in the digital literary sphere, in terms of who generates and negotiates content

---

[108] On the considerably more complex nature of this relationship, and for a specific analysis of the kind of gatekeeping and valorization condensed in literary prizes, see J. F. English, *The Economy of Prestige: Prizes, Awards, and the Circulation of Cultural Value* (Cambridge, MA: Harvard University Press, 2005).

[109] Cf. S. Murray, *The Digital Literary Sphere: Reading, Writing, and Selling Books in the Internet Era* (Baltimore: Johns Hopkins University Press, 2018).

and value. Self-publishing, for example, can circumvent (some) gatekeeping institutions and actors and contribute to diversifying the literary landscape. While the near-monopoly position of big corporations, in particular Amazon, is a huge problem – and measures such as fixed book pricing presumably help to keep this in check – the narratives with which fixed book pricing is promoted, the particular objects and formats it protects, and the underlying concepts of value that it supports, can be misleading or based on archaic and, ultimately, change-averse or diversification-averse views. Thus far, we might read the thriving of the digital literary sphere perhaps not as a process of unmitigated democratization, but instead as a phenomenon that is at least partially symptomatic of the traditional publishing industry's lack of diversity; that is, as symptomatic, also, of the increasing dissatisfaction of writers and readers with white, straight, bourgeois, and so on curating powers. For some time now, the digital literary sphere has enabled a higher degree of porosity and a potential for channeling and enabling alternative valorization, that is, for revalorizing some of the tenets of traditional publishing. This link between alternative valorization and the digital literary sphere brings us to the next section.

3 Are Books *Still* Different? "Difference" in a Digital Age

Even if we agree that books are "different" – and the preceding section has perhaps shown that this is not a straightforward discussion – the past twenty-odd years have wrought changes in the industry that raise the question of "difference" anew within a complex and radically converging media environment. In his recent book *Bitstreams*, Matthew Kirschenbaum writes that "books, by virtue of the bitstream, now share deep ontological commitments and compatibility with other media types, participating in the same technologies and infrastructures and economy." As he continues, "Just as there is nothing unique about the ones and zeros in the bitstream of a book's digital assets, there is also nothing very distinctive about books logistically." He comes to the conclusion that "The air of exceptionalism that has animated so much of the history of the book in other eras vanishes now."[110]

Similarly, the definition of "book" has evolved significantly from the traditional codex format, from "tree flakes encased in dead cow."[111] The policymakers to whom we referred in Section 2 have already been grappling with the extension of their policies to e-books, and yet the book in the digital literary sphere significantly exceeds those *.epub* or *.pdf* versions of the printed book in the list of a traditional publisher. In his white paper "The Business of Books 2019. Publishing in the age of the attention economy,"[112] Rüdiger Wischenbart observes that in examinations and aggregations of sales figures and authors, self-published books and e-books are often ignored. Most certainly, this will be the case for books sold via online subscription and distribution models, and those sold via Amazon Publishing or Kindle Direct. Leaving out these formats runs

---

[110] M. G. Kirschenbaum, *Bitstreams: The Future of Digital Literary Heritage* (Philadelphia: University of Pennsylvania Press, 2021), p. 81.

[111] W. Mitchell, qtd. in D. Finkelstein and A. McCleery, *Introduction to Book History*, 2nd ed. (London: Routledge, 2012), p. 2.

[112] R. Wischenbart, "The Business of Books 2019: Publishing in the Age of the Attention Economy," White paper held at Frankfurter Buchmesse 2019 (2019), p. 5, www.buchmesse.de/files/media/pdf/FBM_BusinessClub_White Paper_2019_0.pdf.

somewhat counter to the staggering numbers of these types of books sold online; after all, more than half of all e-books sold on Amazon are, in fact, self-published, and have proven to be quite lucrative for some authors.[113] The sidelining of subscription models is similarly surprising not least because book clubs, for example, fulfill a central curating function which "is key in an oversaturated market," while they themselves compete in "the market for attention," too.[114] Indeed, in an almost Hobbesian scenario, in the attention economy, different platforms, media, and contributors find themselves "competing against anything and everybody else that connects with the audience."[115] Today, this increasingly means the offerings of the internet and streaming portals as well as more traditional sources such as radio, television, or cinema;[116] Simone Murray circumscribes this complex market as the "contemporary mediasphere" in her book *The Adaptation Industry*,[117] and as Wischenbart concludes in his study, it is a highly

---

[113] Cf. e.g., M. Matting, "Warum eine exklusive Bindung an Amazon via KDP select gut für den Autor ist – und warum nicht," *Die Self-Publisher-Bibel* (November 17, 2020), www.selfpublisherbibel.de/warum-eine-exklusive-bindung-an-amazon-gut-fur-den-autor-ist-und-warum-nicht/; further A. Semuels, "The Authors Who Love Amazon," *The Atlantic* (July 20, 2018), www.theatlantic.com/technology/archive/2018/07/amazon-kindle-unlimited-self-publishing/565664/.

[114] Cf. C. Norrick-Rühl, *Internationaler Buchmarkt* (Frankfurt: Bramann, 2019), p. 70.

[115] In making this point, Wischenbart refers loosely to "Michael Tamblyn: Money on the Table: Opportunities Missed in the eBook Supply Chain. www.michaeltamblyn.com"; R. Wischenbart, "The Business of Books 2019: Publishing in the Age of the Attention Economy," White paper held at Frankfurter Buchmesse 2019 (2019), p. 11, www.buchmesse.de/files/media/pdf/FBM_BusinessClub_WhitePaper_2019_0.pdf.

[116] R. Wischenbart, "The Business of Books 2019: Publishing in the Age of the Attention Economy," White paper held at Frankfurter Buchmesse 2019 (2019), www.buchmesse.de/files/media/pdf/FBM_BusinessClub_WhitePaper_2019_0.pdf.

[117] S. Murray, *The Adaptation Industry: The Cultural Economy of Contemporary Literary Adaptation* (New York: Routledge, 2012).

"competitive environment in which [. . .] reading must find its place or risk marginalisation."[118]

Given these deep shifts in understanding books, creativity, and reading, it seems that the "rise of the novel," erstwhile reduced by Ian Watt to the white, male circle of Defoe, Richardson, and Fielding, and later extended by heterodox scholars first to include women's numerous, prolific, and often widely read works, and currently also those by writers of color, might yet again need to be rewritten: not only are online streaming formats serious competition for attention, they are also formally and aesthetically trespassing into *novel* (in both senses of the word) territory, given that such productions as *The Wire* (David Simon; 2002–2008) are apparently viewed to be "akin to a '60 hour novel' (Griffin 2007) or the 'contemporary equivalent of a Dickens novel' (Mittell 2015: 323)."[119] Kyle Bishop goes as far as suggesting that "TV serials *are* novels"[120] and Netflix's successful political drama *House of Cards* (Beau Willimon; 2013–2018) "called its individual episodes 'chapters;' so does the same service's 1980s-set nostalgia horror series *Stranger Things*" (The Duffer Brothers; 2016–).[121] As one might therefore argue, thinking of literature from the perspective of the attention economy means flattening literature's/books' supposed "difference," even formally and aesthetically. In addition, it seems that the makers of nonliterary genres ("literary" understood in a narrow sense) seek to

---

[118] R. Wischenbart, "The Business of Books 2019: Publishing in the Age of the Attention Economy," White paper held at Frankfurter Buchmesse 2019 (2019), p. 4, www.buchmesse.de/files/media/pdf/FBM_BusinessClub_WhitePaper_2019_0.pdf.

[119] Lanzendörfer, T., and Norrick-Rühl, C, *The Novel as Network: Forms, Ideas, Commodities* (London: Palgrave Macmillan, 2020), p. 6.

[120] Qtd. in T. Lanzendörfer and C. Norrick-Rühl, "Introduction: The Novel as Network," in *The Novel as Network: Forms, Ideas, Commodities*, ed. T. Lanzendörfer and C. Norrick-Rühl (London: Palgrave Macmillan, 2020), p. 6, emphasis added.

[121] T. Lanzendörfer and C. Norrick-Rühl, "Introduction: The Novel as Network," in *The Novel as Network: Forms, Ideas, Commodities*, ed. T. Lanzendörfer and C. Norrick-Rühl (London: Palgrave Macmillan, 2020), p. 6.

capitalize on the appropriation of literary markers, their unique formal qualities, and symbolic capital.

Befitting the shifting grounds of both publishing and form, John B. Thompson has framed digitization as a "revolution not in the product but rather in the process."[122] In a particularly convincing take, he notes that "technologies never act on their own: [...] they are resources that are developed and deployed by actors seeking to pursue their interests and aims in particular social contexts, actors who are using technologies and seizing the opportunities opened up by them to pursue or develop something that they value or deem worthwhile."[123] As such, he reasons: "The social reality of technological change in any industry – and especially an old media industry like book publishing – is a messy affair that is inseparably bound up with power and conflict, as the pursuit of new opportunities by some is often at someone else's expense."[124]

This power-ridden and conflicting nature of human interaction truly emerges in current debates surrounding fixed book pricing – often positioned as a bulwark against change, namely digitization and/or Amazon – just as much as it emerges in current debates surrounding the lack of diversity in the publishing industry. How books and literature are presented in the debate, whether it is series producers claiming their productions resemble novels or more traditional publishers pronouncing on the uniqueness of the (traditionally published) book and/or (brick-and-mortar) bookstores, it is clear that what is at stake is not only the potential loss of a cultural form of unique aesthetic features and haptic reading, kept in qualitative check by knowledgeable gatekeepers ("publishers are different"). It also becomes apparent that existing structures and institutions in publishing are the result of long-term processes of consolidation, of interests, privileges, and particular views, formed by convention, of what is

---

[122] J. B. Thompson, *Book Wars: The Digital Revolution in Publishing* (London: Polity Press, 2021), p. 12.

[123] J. B. Thompson, *Book Wars: The Digital Revolution in Publishing* (London: Polity Press, 2021), p. 475.

[124] J. B. Thompson, *Book Wars: The Digital Revolution in Publishing* (London: Polity Press, 2021), p. 475.

valuable. Indeed, for anyone in literary studies schooled in the shifting views of what makes a culturally valuable "canon" (erstwhile all-white, predominantly male and originating in a particular class), it is out of the question that any form of public promotion or intervention might be neutral, or capable of selecting writers, topics, or genres in a "neutral" way. Judgment – and curation of content – simply is not assigned in a bias-free way. Anecdotal evidence of this from publishing includes instances in which white editors expect Black writers to treat Blackness as "issue-y" or "the problem," as mentioned.[125]

To add an intersectional view, it is worthy of note that initiatives promoting diversification and unlearning racial bias in publishing are often woman-led, as emerged for example from a recent symposium hosted by the Centre for British Studies at HU Berlin.[126] Not only is this an indicator for the gendered component of encouraging diversification in the publishing business (because gender privilege is real and yet often invisible to those privileged), it is also another context in which those who remain underrepresented (women) are expected to do the work of diversification.

Are Books Still Different? Are publishers (still) different? Perhaps the right question would be: Are they already different *enough*, considering the extent of market privilege allocated to the book industry in so many countries? So far, at least to some extent, it seems that the digital literary sphere has capitalized on those aspects of orthodox publishing that make bringing to market a book a complicated, perhaps even exclusivist effort, one that is considerably easier for some authors than it is for others, with the argument that publishers curate quality only cutting so far: where "quality"

---

[125] Cf. for more detail A. Saha and S. van Lente, *RE:Thinking "Diversity" in Publishing* (London: Goldsmith Press, 2020), p. 15, www.spreadtheword.org.uk/wp-content/uploads/2020/06/Rethinking_diversity_in-publishing_WEB.pdf.

[126] Noted by participant Nikola Richter in a comment during the event. Cf. the full program here: "Rethinking 'Diversity' in Publishing: British and German Perspectives," Updated Programme, Humboldt-Universität zu Berlin, www.gbz.hu-berlin.de/downloads/pdf/rethinking-diversity_germany-and-uk_updated-programme_23-april.pdf/view.

or "talent" are pronounced on by a relatively homogenous group, the result will be less reflective of "quality across the board" than it might be. Queer persons who witnessed the rise of the internet in the 1990s and were lucky enough to have access to the infrastructure perhaps at some point read queer fanfiction online and found nooks and crannies bestowing visibility on queer lives; they might have had access to materials, including positive and thus empowering narratives, that were often absent from public discourse (not to mention your nearest brick-and-mortar village book-store). For sure, the queer digital literary sphere has thrived in the shadows of a publishing industry that was, and often continues to be, curated by the standards of heteronormativity and whiteness – and the digital literary sphere continues to play to its full potential in more intersectional configurations, such as in representing Black queer lives or Black women. This eventually will lead us back, in this Element, to Evaristo and what would appear to be her sudden, soaring rise to the skies of public attention and valuation – though this ultimately was, of course, a much longer process and the result of a long, hard campaign that she fought for herself and others.

There is, then, a political aspect to the rise of the digital literary sphere, closely linked to diversification – or: "difference" – that is worth telling and worth consulting. In particular, this political aspect challenges us into rethinking how the genealogy of digitization should be framed. One notable aspect to stress from the interdisciplinary book studies/literary studies perspective applied here is the fact that the onset of the digitization process overlapped with the rise of feminist, postcolonial, queer, and so forth critique from, roughly, the 1980s onwards. It is when these kinds of heterodox approaches began to gain traction in the 1990s, that the impact of digitization on publishing and the book trade also became palpable. Writers began to experiment with forms unique to this new technological apparatus, such as the hyperlink, in digital literatures from the 1980s, that is, even before the World Wide Web was launched in 1993.[127] John Keene also

---

[127] P. Ray Murray, "The Digital Book," in *The Cambridge History of the Book in Britain. Vol. 7: The Twentieth Century and Beyond*, ed. A. Nash, C. Squires, and I. R. Willison (Cambridge: Cambridge University Press, 2019), p. 94.

refs to "a large and growing body of works that initially appeared as far back as the early 1970s, particularly in terms of the earliest cyber poetries, which saw their heyday during the 1990s and first decade of the twentieth century."[128] When it did arrive, the internet "allowed more authors the space to write, publish, and share their own work, to link externally to content, and to push the boundaries of the form."[129] We are now in a situation where "[o]n websites, blogs, newsfeeds, and media streams, a reading-literate culture has transitioned into a writing-dominant culture – and while most bloggers and posters achieve very little in the way of audience numbers, the costs of reaching them are so greatly diminished by digital tools that many have no need of a publisher to package their message."[130] Ranging from download flatrates for e-books to online book clubs, from self-publishing to readers-turned-authors and vice versa, the digital literary sphere is one that is rendering obsolete many of the erstwhile core mechanisms of both authorship and publishing. It does away, at least partially, with the symbolic capital consolidated in publishing. In Simone Murray's words:

> Bourdieu's *The Field of Cultural Production* (1993) and *The Rules of Art* (1996) trace a literary field whose agents are overwhelmingly elite actors collectively possessing a virtual monopoly on the award of symbolic capital in the form of access to publication, literary prizes and critical endorsements. By contrast, it is precisely the contemporary digital literary sphere's mass democratic accessibility, its vocal celebration of amateur self-expression, and the preponderance of

[128] J. Keene, "The Work of Black Literature in the Age of Digital Reproducibility," *Obsidian*, 41 (2015), 1/2: 288–315, www.jstor.org/stable/44489472.

[129] P. Ray Murray, "The Digital Book," in *The Cambridge History of the Book in Britain. Vol. 7: The Twentieth Century and Beyond*, ed. A. Nash, C. Squires, and I. R. Willison (Cambridge: Cambridge University Press, 2019), p. 94.

[130] R. L. Skains, *Digital Authorship: Publishing in the Attention Economy* (Cambridge: Cambridge University Press, 2019), p. 2, www.cambridge.org/core/elements/abs/digital-authorship/C47B1D69263C882BFFC20DFD9F290F38.

born-digital start-ups that generate its cultural energy and
dynamism.[131]

In a similar vein, Skains speaks of "the *demotic author*: one who is 'of the
people'" and "eschews the top-down communication flow of author → text
→ reader in favor of publishing platforms that permit and encourage
feedback and conversation, such as blogs, fanfiction communities and social
media."[132] And for Ramdarshan Bold, "Despite many doomsayers predict-
ing the demise of the book trade, [. . .] the development of the media has
created many new opportunities for, existing and emerging, authors and
consumers of content."[133] In particular, Wattpad as a platform has been
lauded for its inclusivity and the opportunities it affords. Yet it is also a
platform in flux, and now offers a "Paid Stories" program as well as its own
publishing imprint for printed books "Wattpad Books." It remains to be
seen how Wattpad will develop vis-à-vis questions of "demotic authorship," if we remain in Skains' parsing. Ultimately, despite the many

---

[131] S. Murray, *The Digital Literary Sphere: Reading, Writing and Selling Books in the
Internet Era* (Baltimore: Johns Hopkins University Press, 2018), p. 18.

[132] R. L. Skains, *Digital Authorship: Publishing in the Attention Economy*
(Cambridge: Cambridge University Press, 2019), pp. 2–3, www.cambridge
.org/core/elements/abs/digital-authorship/C47B1D69263C882BFFC20D
FD9F290F38.

[133] M. Ramdarshan Bold, "The Return of the Social Author," *Convergence: The
International Journal of Research into New Media Technologie*s, 24 (2018), 2: 117–
136, p. 118: While Wattpad continues to thrive, it is also important to see that
"Some traditional publishers are beginning to embrace self-publishing by devel-
oping their own self-publishing imprints and scouting for talent among other
self-publishing platforms (Phillips, 2014). However, these publisher-led initiatives have not always been popular or successful: the demise of HarperCollins'
writing platform Authonomy, the failing of Penguin Random House's Author
Solutions, the Twitter controversy surrounding HarperCollins' decision to sell
teen writing platform Inkpop to a rival company and concerns around the
commercialization of fan fiction suggest that participatory cultures of creation
do not work under corporate publishing structures (de Kosnik, 2009, Mance,
2015, Page, 2015)."

opportunities to be an author on the World Wide Web, the terrain is highly contested. As Simone Murray wrote in her brief intervention on "10 Myths About Digital Literary Culture": "Digital self-publishing platforms make it easier than ever to see your work in print, but the spoils of publishers' shrinking marketing and publicity budgets fall to established celebrity authors."[134] Hence, while it is important to acknowledge the possibilities afforded by self-publishing[135] and writing platforms, there are also sizable complications, both in terms of remaining bias (as mentioned) and regarding intersections between marketing and power.[136]

Murray's observations already reveal the extent to which the digital literary sphere is heavily influenced by the logics of marketing.[137] There are, admittedly, new opportunities afforded to marketing in the digital literary sphere. On the one hand, new avenues of contact with readers (and potential book-buyers) have opened up through Instagram, TikTok, Goodreads, and so on, and booksellers have proven adept at harnessing their "traditional skills" as "shop-floor booksellers into an online world."[138] On the other hand, marketing budgets are stretched thinner than ever and certain "big books" steal the spotlight and monopolize readers' attention – and budgets. An example of a book which recently received a massive

---

[134] S. Murray, "10 Myths about Digital Literary Culture," *Post45* (August 4, 2020), https://post45.org/2020/04/10-myths-about-digital-literary-culture/.

[135] Cf. also, for contexts, S. Carolan and C. Evain, "Self-Publishing: Opportunities and Threats in a New Age of Mass Culture," *Publishing Research Quarterly*, 29 (2013), 4: 285–300, https://doi.org/10.1007/s12109-013-9326-3.

[136] For more context, see e.g., S. Murray, "Secret Agents: Algorithmic Culture, Goodreads and Datafication of the Contemporary Book World," *European Journal of Cultural Studies*, 24 (2021), 4: 970–989, https://doi.org/10.1177/1367549419886026.

[137] For more context, cf. A. Baverstock and S. Bowen, *How to Market Books* (New York: Routledge, 2019), which covers the theory and practice of marketing books today.

[138] Cf. S. Bayley, "BookTok Giving Bookshops a Boost Not Seen since Rowling, Says Daunt," *The Bookseller* (January 31, 2022), www.thebookseller.com/news/booktok-giving-bookshops-boost-not-seen-rowling-says-daunt-1302475?utm_source=Adestra.

marketing campaign across all channels is Sally Rooney's *Beautiful World, Where Are You?* With exorbitantly high sales expectations, especially in the millennial age group, the book was published in multiple languages at the same time, the type of logistically challenging and expensive "product drop" or "rollout" one usually sees in other creative industries such as for Hollywood blockbusters. The book's look was broadcast across social media and traditional media, leading Dan Sheehan in the *Literary Hub* to (semi-ironically) claim in September 2021 that "Sally Rooney's new novel is now the most reviewed book of all time."[139] Without debating the merits of the book, it is nonetheless important to consider how these "big books" – we really should say "blockbuster books" – such as Rooney's novel use up resources in the attention economy.

The second issue is more complex, and entangled with exclusionary tendencies already in existence in publishing and the wider media landscape that do not just disappear when media transition into digital formats. As digital race scholars observe, the white power structures invested in (and profiting from) the technologies and marketing structures remain a central caveat in any positive notion of the digital sphere.[140] Regarding racism and systemic exclusion in the industry, there is an obvious example of a "blockbuster book" that not only used up valuable resources in the attention economy but also triggered viral discussions about problematic books and cultural appropriation: Jeanine Cummins' *American Dirt* (published in early 2020). The dramatic story of publishing, power, and prejudice has been untangled in several places, most recently and expertly by Sánchez Prado[141]

---

[139] D. Sheehan, "Sally Rooney's New Novel Is Now the Most Reviewed Book of All Time," *Literary Hub* (September 17, 2021), https://lithub.com/sally-rooneys-new-novel-is-now-the-most-reviewed-book-of-all-time/.

[140] Cf. e.g., A. Saha, *Race, Culture and Media* (London: Sage, Kindle ed., 2021); or, earlier, T. Senft and S. Noble, "Race and Social Media," in *The Social Media Handbook*, ed. J. Hunsinger and T. Senft (New York: Routledge, 2013), pp. 107–125.

[141] I. M. Sánchez Prado, "Commodifying Mexico: On *American Dirt* and the Cultural Politics of a Manufactured Bestseller," *American Literary History*, 33 (Summer 2021), 2: 371–393, https://doi.org/10.1093/alh/ajab039.

and by Paisley Rekdal in her book *Appropriate*.[142] Suffice it to say here that this highly anticipated book which was originally seen as giving a voice to underrepresented minorities, and originally marketed as having been written by an author with (partial) Latinx heritage, experienced an unprecedented downfall from critical favor. In an odd twist, it seems that many readers were confronted with publishing's marketing strategies for the first time. As Daniel Hernandez underscores, readers were aggrieved when they saw through the hyper-commodification of "blockbuster books" and realized that *American Dirt* "was poised to be a blockbuster long before copies arrived in bookstores."[143] Even if readers were disappointed to see that literature was treated more like a commodity than culture, the book still, unwittingly, achieved bestseller status.[144] There is, anecdotally speaking, no such thing as bad publicity when only considering sales figures, at least not for the big conglomerate publishers who can weather a social media storm, though even large publishers have recently had their hands forced by social media discussions.[145]

---

[142] Cf. P. Rekdal, *Appropriate: A Provocation* (New York: WW Norton, 2021), pp. 71–91.

[143] D. Hernandez, "'American Dirt' Was Supposed to Be a Publishing Triumph: What Went Wrong?" *Los Angeles Times* (January 26, 2020), www.latimes.com/entertainment-arts/story/2020-01-26/american-dirt-publishing-latino-representation.

[144] L. Shapiro, "Blurbed to Death: How One of Publishing's Most Hyped Books Became its Biggest Horror Story – and Still Ended Up a Best Seller," *Vulture* (January 5, 2021), www.vulture.com/article/american-dirt-jeanine-cummins-book-controversy.html.

[145] For instance, there have been a number of recent cases in which titles have been taken off the list or even pulped due to allegations of sexual indecency against the authors. For more details, see C. Koegler, C. Norrick-Rühl, P. Pohlmann, and G. Sieg, "'Must Writers Be Moral?': Interdisziplinäre Perspektiven auf 'Morality Clauses' im Literaturbetrieb," in *Literatur und Recht: Materialität: Formen und Prozesse gegenseitiger Vergegenständlichung*, ed. E. Achermann, A. Blödorn, P. Pohlmann, and C. Norrick-Rühl (Berlin: De Gruyter, forthcoming).

Blockbuster marketing is something that only big conglomerate publishers can afford, and only very irregularly at that. Smaller and mid-size publishers have to find other avenues and be more creative to achieve visibility and reach readers. Claire Squires and Beth Driscoll recently analyzed the ecologies of neoliberal publishing by focusing on the differences between large and small publishers and their visibility at Frankfurt Book Fair, using the terms "megativity" and "miniaturization" to grasp the differences between conglomerate publishing and micropublishing. Anecdotally, even successful small publishers like Galley Beggar Press cannot afford a booth at Frankfurt Book Fair, so they buy a trade visitor ticket and find spaces and places to hold meetings in communal fair areas.[146] Nonetheless, it seems that some micro-, small, and mid-size publishers have found ways to carve out their niche, and serve previously underserved readers. As Ann Steiner recently observed, the book industry today is a "polarized market, where the largest publishing houses dominate, but it has simultaneously made space for micropublishers, self-publishing, small independent presses, and the like, whose titles cross borders in ways that owe little to traditional, national, book market patterns."[147] In some ways, the new affordances of the digital era have made publishing a less insecure business venture, or at least entrepreneurship in publishing a more feasible prospect, since the start-up costs have decreased.[148] Developments like easier e-book production, digital printing, print-on-demand, or crowdfunding platforms like Publishizer.com[149] have opened up possibilities to reach and serve niche readers.

[146] For more anecdotes and observations, see B. Driscoll and C. Squires, "Megativity and Miniaturization at the Frankfurt Book Fair," *Post45* (August 4, 2020), https://post45.org/2020/04/megativity-and-miniaturization-at-the-frankfurt-book-fair/.

[147] A. Steiner, "The Global Book: Micropublishing, Conglomerate Production, and Digital Market structures," *Publishing Research Quarterly*, 34 (2018): 118–132, https://link.springer.com/article/10.1007/s12109-017-9558-8.

[148] R. Noorda, *Entrepreneurial Identity in US Book Publishing in the Twenty-First Century* (Cambridge: Cambridge University Press, 2021), p. 27, www.cambridge.org/core/elements/entrepreneurial-identity-in-us-book-publishing-in-the-twentyfirst-century/BA08F39C6C448AB1544D292E61F2B85A.

[149] Publishizer, https://publishizer.com/.

As Jenni Ramone has shown, the bonuses of the digital literary sphere can be spread far and wide. For instance, thanks to the global marketplace created (and controlled[150]) by Amazon, small Nigerian presses such as "Cassava Republic and Parresia are able to compete with global publishers online, meaning that alongside the celebrated migrant Nigerian authors writing for a global audience, more 'locally' inflected Nigerian literary texts are finding a route to a broader literary market."[151] Of course, there are promising examples like these which offer a "silver lining" view of the market dominance of Amazon and major conglomerates. But in comparison to corporate publishing, the potential for large-scale success is limited. As Simone Murray states, even in the digital literary sphere, "some authors are more equal than others."[152] As Rachel Noorda details in her recent Cambridge Element in this series on entrepreneurial identity in US publishing,

> booksellers and publishers are middlemen in a time when the digital literary sphere[89] is such that authors can reach readers directly if desired, without the assistance of publishers or booksellers. However, publishers and booksellers still add value to the book industry by providing editorial, design and marketing work to shape and promote a manuscript, and to make that manuscript visible and accessible to a larger audience.

Noorda emphasizes, "Publishers and booksellers also act as gatekeepers and legitimizing forces in the industry, where getting a publishing contract with

---

[150] Cf. e.g., P. Sehgal, "All You Can Read: Is Amazon Changing the Novel," *The New Yorker* (November 1, 2021), pp. 75–78, here p. 76.

[151] J. Ramone, *Postcolonial Literatures in the Local Literary Marketplace* (London: Palgrave Macmillan, Kindle ed., 2020), p. 87.

[152] S. Murray, "10 Myths about Digital Literary Culture," *Post45* (August 4, 2020), https://post45.org/2020/04/10-myths-about-digital-literary-culture/#footnote_3_11542.

a publisher or seeing their book in a bookstore is often sought by the author as a means of legitimizing their work."[153]

Besides the replication of existing inequalities in the digital sphere, digital spaces also, unfortunately, offer spaces for new forms of harassment and bullying, also known as trolling.[154] Mark Davis goes so far as to speak of an "online 'anti-public sphere'" – spaces in which tone "routinely and radically flouts the ethical and rational norms of democratic discourse."[155] These have burgeoned and become more visible in the digital era. Research has shown that women, especially women of color, are at a particular risk of being targeted. At a workshop in Münster, Germany, a social media manager for a major conglomerate-owned German trade publisher disclosed, for instance, that certain authors in their list have chosen to abstain from social media because they feel that the Internet is not a safe space for women of color.[156] This indicates that the idea of "putting yourself out there" as an author does not mean the same thing for every author, depending on profile and identity. Certain types of texts are also more likely to draw criticism and trolling than authors. A German author of color who has repeatedly pointed out how difficult this balancing act is for women on the Internet is Jasmina Kuhnke, who also highlighted discussions about right-wing radicalism at Frankfurt Book Fair in October 2021.[157]

---

[153] R. Noorda, *Entrepreneurial Identity in US Book Publishing in the Twenty-First Century* (Cambridge: Cambridge University Press, 2021), p. 31, www.cambridge.org/core/elements/entrepreneurial-identity-in-us-book-publishing-in-the-twentyfirst-century/BA08F39C6C448AB1544D292E61F2B85A.

[154] Cf. S. Murray, *The Digital Literary Sphere: Reading, Writing, and Selling Books in the Internet Era* (Baltimore: Johns Hopkins University Press, 2018), p. 123.

[155] M. Davis, "The Online Anti-Public Sphere," *European Journal of Cultural Studies*, 24 (2021), 1: 143–159, p. 143, https://doi.org/10.1177/1367549420902799.

[156] Reported at a workshop held in July 2021 in Münster, Germany.

[157] K. Gottschalk, "Comedy-Autorin über Aktivismus: 'Twitter ist für mich Battle-Rap'," *taz* (October 23, 2021), https://taz.de/Comedy-Autorin-ueber-Aktivismus/!5807195/. For more context, see C. Norrick-Rühl, "Politics at Play in the Kabuff: The Buchmesse as a Political Space," in *The Frankfurt Kabuff Critical Edition*, ed. B. Driscoll and C. Squires (2023, forthcoming).

Literature "is not created equal" in the digital sphere, just as it is not in more traditional publishing. As the literary agent Cherise Fisher illustrates, "There is an engine in publishing houses. Not every book gets the same amount of gas. Some books get premium. Some get regular."[158] Corinna Norrick-Rühl has outlined elsewhere that "some novels [for example] are connected more firmly to central actors and institutions in the marketplace, and thus, their success is often predetermined by and through their level of networkedness."[159] Ultimately this Element is not the place to either analyze or decide the true levels of participatory potential of the digital literary sphere, not least because different platforms are run by different groups who have different scopes for engaging heterodox writers and audiences. And yet, while the digital literary sphere retains the possibility to confer space and availability on heterodox cultural productions and formats of exchange, those readers who remain wary of the limitations of publishing's heading of majority culture can and will move their buyer's power online because they can, thereby putting pressure on the less diverse mainstream.

The intense industry discussions following the murder of George Floyd and the rise of the #BlackLivesMatter protests across the globe in 2020 provide an excellent example of the realignment of value categories in publishing through hashtag activism and internet movements. Seemingly overnight, the digital literary sphere was awash with discussions, recommendations, and comments about the lack of diversity in publishing. The lack of diversity had been acknowledged and measured for years, but the merging of activism and urgency led to new action being taken. For instance, during the following weeks, the

[158] Qtd. in C. de León, A. Alter, E. A. Harris, and J. Khatib, "'A Conflicted Cultural Force': What It's Like to Be Black in Publishing," *The New York Times* (July 1, 2020; Updated June 3, 2021), www.nytimes.com/2020/07/01/books/book-publishing-black.html?action=click&module=RelatedLinks&pgtype=Article.

[159] C. Norrick-Rühl, "Introduction: Novel Commodities," in *The Novel as Network: Forms, Ideas, Commodities*, ed. T. Lanzendörfer and C. Norrick-Rühl (London: Palgrave Macmillan, 2020), p. 205.

hashtag #publishingpaidme highlighted the discrepancies between advances for white authors and advances for BIPOC authors.[160] Amistad Press launched the hashtag #BlackOutBestsellerList to challenge readers to buy any two Black-authored books during a specific week in June 2020, with the goal of demonstrating "our power and clout in the publishing industry."[161] New hires in publishing were widely reported, and media outlets disproportionately shone light on the issue (after years of ignoring and perpetuating the exclusionary practices).[162] New imprints were founded as well, to highlight marginalized voices; one example is Hachette US with Legacy Lit,[163] another is Hachette UK with Dialogue Books.[164] Without elaborating much further here, it could be argued that the names of these imprints hint at the difficulties of trying to solve the diversity problem without creating more spaces for pigeonholing. Simon & Schuster has closed their imprint for Black voices, 37 Ink for this reason. As the incoming editor Dana Canedy (the first Black person to lead Simon & Schuster's signature imprint) explained, "the imprint's existence allowed people to say, 'Oh, that's a 37 Ink book'" when a book by a person of color was pitched. Canedy emphasized that instead of being relegated to one particular imprint "all of the books we acquire by and about people of

[160] A. Flood, "#Publishingpaidme: Authors Share Advances to Expose Racial Disparities," *The Guardian* (June 8, 2020), www.theguardian.com/books/2020/jun/08/publishingpaidme-authors-share-advances-to-expose-racial-disparities.

[161] C. Reid, "Amistad Launches #BlackoutBestsellerList on Social Media," *Publishers Weekly* (June 15, 2020), www.publishersweekly.com/pw/by-topic/industry-news/publisher-news/article/83593-amistad-launches-blackoutbestsellerlist-on-social-media.html.

[162] See, inter alia, R. J. So and G. Wezerek, "Just How White Is the Book Industry?" *The New York Times* (December 11, 2020), www.nytimes.com/interactive/2020/12/11/opinion/culture/diversity-publishing-industry.html.

[163] Legacy Lit, www.legacylitbooks.com/landing-page/meet-legacy-lit/.

[164] Hachette Book Group, https://vip7.hachette.co.uk/imprint/lbbg/dialogue-books/page/little-brown-books/lbbg-imprint-dialogue/.

color should be Simon & Schuster books."[165] There are, predictably, other opinions in the industry which emphasize the value of new imprints for marginalized voices. As the editor of Legacy Lit, Krishan Trotman, explains, trends in the industry can be short-lived: "There will be a huge boom of books – all of a sudden Black women are hot or urban fiction is hot – and then there will be a backslide." She considers the establishment of imprints like Legacy Lit as more lasting: "we need these imprints. They'll be here even after all the hoopla dies down."[166]

It remains to be seen how these new imprints develop and whether they last. In any case, there have been visible and momentous shifts in the publishing industry – one could even say, an "industry reckoning"[167] in 2020 (and not without backlash, as the *New York Times* discussed in 2021[168]). These developments and the media attention they received show how today, wider societal movements, perpetuated through the flattened hierarchies and shifted attention logics in the digital sphere, influence the (digital) literary sphere directly. As we transition to the next section, a case study of Bernardine Evaristo's post-Booker activities, it is central to note that Evaristo herself believes that the recent shifts in publishing, caused by

[165] "I want everyone publishing what would formerly have been thought of as 37 Ink books. Not to say we didn't have books by and about people of color, but all of the books we acquire by and about people of color should be Simon & Schuster books." Qtd. in A. Alter and E. A. Harris, "'There Are Tons of Brown Faces Missing': Publishers Step Up Diversity Efforts," *The New York Times* (October 29, 2020), www.nytimes.com/2020/10/29/books/publishing-diver sity-new-hires.html.

[166] R. J. So and G. Wezerek, "Just How White Is the Book Industry?" *The New York Times* (December 11, 2020), www.nytimes.com/interactive/2020/12/11/opinion/culture/diversity-publishing-industry.html.

[167] C. de León and E. A. Harris, "#PublishingPaidMe and a Day of Action Reveal an Industry Reckoning," *The New York Times* (June 10, 2020), www.nytimes.com/2020/06/08/books/publishingpaidme-publishing-day-of-action.html.

[168] E. A. Harris, "In Backlash to Racial Reckoning, Conservative Publishers See Gold," *The New York Times* (August 15, 2021), www.nytimes.com/2021/08/15/books/race-antiracism-publishing.html.

#MeToo and #BlackLivesMatter, provided fertile ground for her Booker win. She has, in the past, effectively used the internet and social media to further her cultural agenda, as she describes in regard to the Brunel International African Poetry Prize, which she founded: "I set up a website, called in favours [...], and marketed it via social media."[169] The next section will provide insights into Evaristo's effective handling of literature as culture and commodity in a digital age, and will help us conclude (Section 5) with final remarks on whether and how books, today, are still "different."

[169] B. Evaristo, *Manifesto: On Never Giving Up* (London: Hamish Hamilton, 2021), p. 174.

4 Marketing "Difference" in a Network of Networks: Bernardine Evaristo

In keeping with the ideas developed in our previous section about a broad understanding of the digital literary sphere, we open our case study with a quote from Bernardine Evaristo: "Society operates via powerful & often impenetrable networks that uphold its tribal hierarchies, so we must establish our own systems as countermeasure."[170] The idea of establishing a counternetwork to equalize literary hierarchies and counteract exclusionary practices not only chimes with the "novel as network" metaphor that we have flagged throughout this Element, but also coincides with the "diverse networks of dissent" that have been propagated by scholars concerned with hashtag activism.[171] It further resonates with the kind of affective, transatlantic network[172] that Evaristo envisages as part of her own influences as a writer: women of color, writing from different sides of the Atlantic:

> Black women writers were the ones I needed to read as a very young woman, and I didn't come across any in Britain who were born or raised here and writing our stories from this perspective. My inspiration came from African Americans: Audre Lorde, Toni Morrison, Gloria Naylor and Alice Walker were foremost among them, and of course Ntozake Shange; and the Jamaican-American writer Michelle Cliff, and the Nigerian novelist Buchi Emecheta who had arrived in Britain in 1962 as an adult, and wrote primarily about Nigeria. These were the writers who

---

[170] B. Evaristo, *Manifesto: On Never Giving Up* (London: Hamish Hamilton, 2021), p. 189.

[171] S. J. Jackson, M. Bailey, and B. Foucault Welles, *#HashtagActivism: Networks of Race and Gender Justice* (Cambridge, MA: MIT Press, 2020), p. xxxviii.

[172] Cf. C. Koegler, "Memorialising African Being and Becoming in the Atlantic World: Affective Her-Stories by Yaa Gyasi and Bernardine Evaristo," in *The Routledge Companion to Gender and Affect*, ed. T. W. Reeser (New York: Routledge, 2022), pp. 374–385.

foregrounded black women's lives and in so doing gave me permission to write.[173]

This is an "authorial act of pulling together – across the Atlantic – an empowering and growing archive of black female voices"[174] on the part of Evaristo – a heterodox network that goes back to, as well as diversifies, the Atlantic's own deep archives of forced migration and disenfranchisement. It is a network that extends into the present, conveying to the young Evaristo a sense of voice and "permission"; and eventually, it extends into a range of other networks that have emerged with the internet and are therefore unique to the twenty-first century: the digital literary sphere and social media – Twitter, Facebook, and Instagram. Evaristo has expertly used these networks of the present to push her anti-racist and queer/trans*-inclusive agenda as well as promote her own works and those of fellow writers. A recent example: in 2020 she foreworded a new edition of Beryl Gilroy's *Black Teacher*, a novel she writes "has been overlooked, that's the truth of it, barely making the timelines of black British literary history"[175]; Evaristo is also keenly aware of the extent to which the Windrush writers, from E.R. Braithwaite to Sam Selvon, were able to grab the spotlight in a way that was not possible for Gilroy – who appears to have been the sole female writer among them. Gilroy's "rare perspective of a black woman transported to the colonial motherland"[176] is part of the network that Evaristo is

---

[173] B. Evaristo, *Manifesto: On Never Giving Up* (London: Hamish Hamilton, 2021), p. 158. C. Koegler also discusses this quote in "Memorialising African Being and Becoming in the Atlantic World: Affective Her-Stories by Yaa Gyasi and Bernardine Evaristo," in *The Routledge Companion to Gender and Affect*, ed. T. W. Reeser (New York: Routledge, 2022), pp. 374–385.

[174] C. Koegler, "Memorialising African Being and Becoming in the Atlantic World: Affective Her-Stories by Yaa Gyasi and Bernardine Evaristo," in *The Routledge Companion to Gender and Affect*, ed. T. W. Reeser (New York: Routledge, 2022), pp. 374–385.

[175] B. Evaristo, "Foreword," in B. Gilroy, *Black Teacher* (London: Faber & Faber, Kindle ed., 2021), pp. 8–9.

[176] B. Evaristo, "Foreword," in B. Gilroy, *Black Teacher* (London: Faber & Faber, Kindle ed., 2021), pp. 8–9.

contributing to curate and shape. Her recent book series "Black Britain: Writing Back," published by Hamish Hamilton (Penguin Random House), with thirteen books to date, is another prominent example of this kind of advocacy.[177]

Evaristo's Booker win is part of the cascade effects that are unfolding in the wake of these converging networks, long in the making, and yet in many ways, it was an event of unprecedented significance. As mentioned, Evaristo was the first Black woman to be awarded the prize – the first to emerge from a long archive and a group that had previously often been overlooked both in the industry generally and in prize culture more specifically. According to a *Guardian* study from 2021, "black authors made up 6% of shortlisted authors in the UK's top literary prizes in the past 25 years. Over the same 25-year period, black Britons made up 3.1% of shortlisted nominees"; in addition, "The percentage of black and minority ethnic (BAME) authors increased from 4.65% in 1996 to 34.25% in 2020," though in "the years 1996, 2001, 2002 and 2009 there were no black authors shortlisted across any of the prizes."[178] Along with the Booker prize, the study included "Women's prize for fiction, Folio prize, Orwell book prize, Baillie Gifford, International Dylan Thomas prize, Carnegie medal, and Costa book awards (encompassing Costa first novel award, Costa novel award, Costa biography award, Costa poetry award and Costa children's award)."[179] Toni Morrison, who won the Nobel Prize in 1993, is an important predecessor, of course, though her example is also eye-opening regarding the fierce policing forces emanating from hegemonic whiteness,

---

[177] Penguin, Black Britain: Writing Back Series, www.penguin.co.uk/series/ bbwb/black-britain–writing-back.html.

[178] A. Mohdin, T. Thomas, G. Quach, and Z. Šeško, "One in Five Shortlisted Authors for Top UK Literary Prizes in 2020 were Black," *The Guardian* (October 1, 2021), www.theguardian.com/world/2021/oct/01/shortlisted-authors-uk-literary-prizes-black-diversity.

[179] A. Mohdin, T. Thomas, G. Quach, and Z. Šeško, "One in Five Shortlisted Authors for Top UK Literary Prizes in 2020 were Black," *The Guardian* (October 1, 2021), www.theguardian.com/world/2021/oct/01/shortlisted-authors-uk-literary-prizes-black-diversity.

given that she would be asked for decades to come when she would finally start addressing topics beyond the "niche" world of Black lives.[180] These are paradoxical expectations, of course, given that BIPOC writers so often also have been under pressure to reinvoke white fantasies about Black lives, such as those centered on crime, social issues, and so forth, as already mentioned. This brings us back to the "nonthreatening" ways in which Black lives have been allowed, if at all, to emerge into the white-hegemonic sphere of public attention. Morrison's early insistence on their validity, particularly depicting also the suffering that Black people have endured at the hands of whites, was a marked exception.

As Catherine Knight Steele writes in *Digital Black Feminism*, "Dual subordination based on both race and gender prohibits full access to the process of self-naming for Black women";[181] however – and this is of particular significance for this Element – "the digital environment provides an opportunity to resist external naming structures and controlling images of Black women."[182] This is partially because of how digital networks work themselves, that is, because "Socially mediated environments *require* acts of naming for participation."[183] In this context, Steele perceives a clear, at times problematic proximity between "naming as a liberatory practice" and "branding as a financial necessity for Black women" which she terms "a relatively short walk"[184] though there is a clear sense in her own work and that of others that the empowering potentials of the digital sphere for heterodox voices, and their overlaps with self-branding, are undeniable, given that "digital Black feminists demonstrate their skill in designing

[180] Cf. H. Wabuke, "'Manifesto' is a Story of Dreams Made Real by Never Giving Up," *NPR* (January 18, 2022), www.npr.org/2022/01/18/1073739054/manifesto-is-a-story-of-dreams-made-real-by-never-giving-up?.

[181] C. K. Steele, *Digital Black Feminism* (New York: New York University Press, Kindle ed., 2021), p. 131.

[182] C. K. Steele, *Digital Black Feminism* (New York: New York University Press, Kindle ed., 2021), p. 131.

[183] C. K. Steele, *Digital Black Feminism* (New York: New York University Press, Kindle ed., 2021), p. 131, our emphasis.

[184] C. K. Steele, *Digital Black Feminism* (New York: New York University Press, Kindle ed., 2021), p. 131, our emphasis.

brands for themselves online."[185] Illuminating yet another direction in which the circuits of Black dissent potentially extend, Anna Everett perceives a "short walk" of another kind, one that extends historically: drawing on scholars of the Black Atlantic from Braithwaite to Paul Gilroy, Everett has focused on technological aspects of Black resistance since the plantationocene, tying this in with the notion of "virtual communities":

> Despite the well-documented dehumanizing imperatives of the colonial encounter, the ethnically and nationally diverse Africans in the New World developed self-sustaining *virtual communities* through paralinguistic and transnational communicative systems and networks of song, dance, talking drums, and other musical instrumentations. The formation of these new African-inflected communication strategies enabled this heterogeneous mass of people somehow to overcome their profound dislocation, fragmentation, alienation, relocation, and ultimate commodification in the Western slavocracies of the modern world.[186]

Twenty years later, Kelly Baker Josephs and Roopika Risam reinstate this proximity, even convergence, between these much older virtual forms and current digital activism, emphasizing the *longue durée* of technophilic Black resistance: "Black people have always been intimately familiar with technologies, both repressive and emancipatory – whether the ship, musical instruments, games, social media, or algorithms."[187] In this context, it is important to acknowledge particularly the role that Black women have

---

[185] C. K. Steele, *Digital Black Feminism* (New York: New York University Press, Kindle ed., 2021), p. 18.

[186] A. Everett, "The Revolution Will Be Digitized: Afrocentricity and the Digital Public Sphere," *Social Text*, 20 (2002), 2: 125–146, https://muse.jhu.edu/article/31928.

[187] K. B. Josephs and R. Risam, "Introduction: The Digital Black Atlantic," in *The Digital Black Atlantic*, ed. R. Risam and K. B. Josephs (Minneapolis: University of Minnesota Press, Kindle ed., 2021), p. ix, our emphasis.

played. For example, it is one of Steele's pronounced goals in *Digital Black Feminism* to "reposition Black women online as purveyors of digital skill and expertise, not deficient or in need of new skills to survive a changing digital landscape"; to give examples that highlight Black women who "without extensive programming experience have maximized platform affordances, built transmedia platforms, led platform migrations, pushed platform policy changes regarding hate speech and content moderation, and introduced us to new pay structures as precursors to influencer culture."[188] Her positive and agency-focused treatment of Black women's usage and transformation of digital technology also extends to this usage's overlaps with branding, just as it overlaps with the sense that Black labor deserves valuation and financial compensation, particularly given that "Black women are ignored as intellectuals and experts."[189] "[T]hey reclaim self-branding as an agentic practice," Steele writes, not least because many "are naming themselves through their brand and relying on Black oral traditions like signifyin' to deploy a Black feminist brand online intentionally."[190] While Steele does signal concern about the limited transgressiveness of "[c]lickable and hashtaggable Black feminism,"[191] she refuses to undermine digital Black feminism's empowering potential, including where its overlaps with branding and self-branding become entirely overt. The two simply are not mutually exclusive.

It is possible to situate Evaristo's authorship-*cum*-activism – online and offline, current and historical – and the events of 2019 against this backdrop of converging networks. The Booker prize 2019 was not only bestowed on a novel that celebrates a large variety of Black female (including nonbinary) voices and their diverse links with Atlantic displacements and/or

---

[188] C. K. Steele, *Digital Black Feminism* (New York: New York University Press, Kindle ed., 2021), p. 2.

[189] C. K. Steele, *Digital Black Feminism* (New York: New York University Press, Kindle ed., 2021), p. 138.

[190] C. K. Steele, *Digital Black Feminism* (New York: New York University Press, Kindle ed., 2021), p. 132.

[191] C. K. Steele, *Digital Black Feminism* (New York: New York University Press, Kindle ed., 2021), p. 135.

journeys – *Girl, Woman, Other*; it also was an event that was shared with readers in the digital sphere more widely than in previous years. Integrating announcements posted on YouTube on the Booker's dedicated channel, TheBookerPrizes,[192] Evaristo's win was advertised widely across social media. A closer look at the Booker videos in January 2022 shows that the YouTube announcements did not garner much attention in 2019 – for instance, the longlist video announcement has only tallied just under 4,000 views to date (posted in July 2019),[193] and the prize announcement also only has approximately 4,000 views (posted in October 2019).[194] Evaristo's shortlist video has only received 2,035 views (posted in October 2019)[195] – though this is significantly higher than Atwood's shortlist video, which has only tallied 733 views to date.[196] Compared to these numbers, the more recent videos, posted in 2020 and 2021, have garnered much more attention. Of course, this is only anecdotal evidence and should not be over-interpreted. However, one possible interpretation could be that the COVID-19 pandemic changed the way the Booker used their own channel (established in 2008, currently at 6.72K subscribers and 908K views overall[197]), driving more

---

[192] TheBookerPrizes [Channel], *YouTube*, www.youtube.com/channel/UCx0g6-WY4RMUBM9j2PmFusA.

[193] TheBookerPrizes, "The 2019 Booker Prize Longlist Announced [Video]," *YouTube* (July 24, 2019), www.youtube.com/watch?v=9DS17Q 1zf64&list=PLf5wOwLcmpzmF-7Bdeaw13e8kToXD7Uoq&index=1.

[194] TheBookerPrizes, "The 2019 Booker Prize Winners Announced [Video]," *YouTube* (October 14, 2019), www.youtube.com/watch?v=bgGTJgIO0Uc& list=PLf5wOwLcmpzmF-7Bdeaw13e8kToXD7Uoq&index=10.

[195] TheBookerPrizes, "2019 Booker Prize Shortlist Author Video – Bernardine Evaristo [Video]," *YouTube* (October 14, 2019), www.youtube.com/watch? v=jb7j-ZoUN4M&list=PLf5wOwLcmpzmF-7Bdeaw13e8kToXD7Uo q&index=4.

[196] TheBookerPrizes, "2019 Booker Prize Shortlist Author Video – Margaret Atwood [Video]," *YouTube* (October 16, 2019), www.youtube.com/watch? v=4iLY9TExq2Q&list=PLf5wOwLcmpzmF-7Bdeaw13e8kToXD7Uoq& index=8.

[197] Stats as of January 2022. Cf. TheBookerPrizes [Channel], "About," *YouTube*, www.youtube.com/c/TheBookerPrizes/about.

traffic there. It may also be indicative of a heightened awareness of the digital literary sphere among readers in the pandemic era, due to the lack of in-person alternatives.[198] For comparison, the 2020 longlist announcement (posted in July 2020), has over 10,000 views;[199] and the 2021 longlist announcement (posted in July 2021) has just over 5,000 views.[200] The Booker Prize YouTube channel has become more central to the prize's branding, due to pandemic-induced contact regulations and lockdowns, but this has also brought the Booker closer to a wider and perhaps, following Evaristo's win, also more inclusive and diverse readership, which might be one reason for the significantly higher numbers, though it is too soon to tell in earnest where the prize is heading. Certainly, until 2018, the Booker still was very much in a mode of gatekeeping, celebrating its own "exclusionary, inequitable" approach with exclusive, ticketed events, as criticized for instance by Stevie Marsden in her *Medium* article "Why I'm done with the Man Booker and you should be too."[201] As such, Evaristo's Booker win might be considered not only a watershed moment for her own career and Black women writers more generally, but also for the Booker as a gatekeeping institution – time will tell.

Evaristo's diversifying, multidirectional approach and its convergence with the publishing and prizing industry can serve to clarify further how literature functions both as culture and commodity in the digital age and if, or to what extent, books might (still) count as different today or not; indeed if the question still matters at all or, if so, in what ways and for whom. In either case, it becomes tantamount that the "digital literary sphere" be understood

---

[198] For observations on the shifts in the creative sector during the pandemic, cf. e.g., M. S. Jeannotte, "When the Gigs Are Gone: Valuing Arts, Culture and Media in the COVID-19 Pandemic," *Social Sciences & Humanities Open*, 3 (2021), 1, 100097, pp. 1–7. https://doi.org/10.1016/j.ssaho.2020.100097.

[199] TheBookerPrizes, "The 2020 Booker Prize Longlist Announcement [Video]," *YouTube* (July 28, 2020), www.youtube.com/watch?v=AYbYLL7lLbM.

[200] TheBookerPrizes, "2021 Booker Prize Longlist Announced [Video]," *YouTube* (July 27, 2021), www.youtube.com/watch?v=PIrKprfwhJM&list=PLf5w OwLcmpzl_vatzqC3p4lKiwsG3d4zv&index=33.

[201] S. Marsden, "Why I'm Done with the Man Booker Prize and You Should Be too," *Medium* (July 10, 2018), https://medium.com/@steviemarsden/why-im-done-with-the-man-booker-prize-and-you-should-be-too-ad0057b95baf.

as an integrated sphere in the widest sense. Not only do we suggest to situate digitally created or sold literature, and the internet's own unique platforms (Wattpad, Publishizer, etc.), as part of the digital literary sphere, but also to conceptually converge the digital literary sphere with a kind of transmediality that further links up to other types of social media, branding, and more traditional cultural practices. These can then be understood as interconnected avenues of influence, narrative, and practice: in a network of networks. In turn, we suggest that it is in variously sourcing and interlinking these, from hashtag activism to novel-writing to website creation, that individual authors shape images of themselves and their work, or push particular narratives and stories that transcend any single medium, in particular that of the traditional "book." Emerging as they do in a symbolic economy of discourse, authors wittingly and unwittingly actualize aspects of performative branding that will interact with and intervene in existing networks and circuits of valuation. In addition, there is no doubt that usage of social media and direct interaction with the digital literary sphere can be a means of pushing *particular* (brand) narratives that potentially very much correspond to core beliefs held by their authors.

The Booker is not only a cultural institution for anglophone literature but it is also itself highly commercialized, something that is underlined, for example, by the fact that the publishers of shortlisted books are required to contribute substantial amounts to offset the marketing costs for the Booker.[202] In particular, though, books that are not highly anticipated to actually win the prize do profit from the attention that the Booker bestows on them – and directs at them. For Evaristo, commercial success did not materialize until after her Booker win. Before, *Girl, Woman, Other* had been in UK bookstores for five months and had only sold a few thousand copies. Despite the usual difficulties in quantifying the sales success triggered by a literary prize,[203] the numbers are

---

[202] Cf. M. Ramdarshan Bold and C. Norrick-Rühl, "The Independent Foreign Fiction Prize and Man Booker International Prize Merger," *Logos*, 28 (2017), 3: 7–24, p. 9, https://doi.org/10.1163/1878-4712-11112131.

[203] Cf. e.g., M. Ramdarshan Bold and C. Norrick-Rühl, "The Independent Foreign Fiction Prize and Man Booker International Prize Merger," *Logos*, 28 (2017), 3: 7–24, pp. 13–14, https://doi.org/10.1163/1878-4712-11112131.

striking: "Five days after her victory for Girl, Woman, Other – her radiant novel about 12 mostly black, mostly female, Britons – [. . .] total sales of the book, which had been in bookshops for five months, [. . .] more than doubled from 4,391 copies sold to 10,371" – an increase of 1,340 percent.[204] To date (February 2022), the book "has sold more than a million copies in English, with deals in thirty-five territories and twenty-nine languages."[205] In several interviews, Evaristo emphasized that she would now finally be making money for her publisher as well. In a *Vanity Fair* interview, she sums up the importance of both her activism and her commercial success succinctly: "I think the way in which the publishing industry changes is through lobbying and activism, something that I've been involved in for many years. I think that books that become an economic success open doors for other writers because publishers are businesses and need to make money."[206] The trailblazing effects of commercially successful pioneers can be beneficial for others, both financially as well as culturally and politically; they lay paths in new directions into which a heterodox network may extend further.

Evaristo thus has clearly been very aware of the commercial pressures in the industry, and also of the necessity of self-marketing, self-branding, and of positioning her books as an attractive commodity, from the beginnings of her writing career onwards. In her memoir-meets-manifesto, she describes her efforts to market her first books on her own, without the financial support of the small press that published her first two books. The book industry, back then, she maintains, was very different than it is now: "Nobody was waiting for my manuscripts,

---

[204] A. Flood, "Bernardine Evaristo Doubles Lifetime Sales in Five Days after Joint Booker Win," *The Guardian* (October 22, 2019), www.theguardian.com/ books/2019/oct/22/bernardine-evaristo-doubles-lifetime-sales-in-five-days-after-joint-booker-win.

[205] A. Russell, "How Bernardine Evaristo Conquered British Literature," *The New Yorker* (February 3, 2022), www.newyorker.com/culture/persons-of-interest/ how-bernardine-evaristo-conquered-british-literature.

[206] A. Tepper, "The Little Book That Could: How Bernardine Evaristo Became an International Writer-to-Watch in 2019," *Vanity Fair* (December 13, 2019), www.vanityfair.com/style/2019/12/bernardine-evaristo-girl-woman-other-interview.

agents weren't seeking out new black talent the way they do now on social media."[207] But instead of resigning herself and her works to a small audience, she actively marketed the books, despite the fact that she hadn't even received advance payments for her books and was reliant solely on royalties for income: "I hustled," she writes, "I paid to print up thousands of leaflets advertising it [*Lara*], which I posted via the mail-outs of arts and literature organizations, who charged a fee for the service."[208] This self-marketing paid off. While her first two books were hardly noticed by national media, her third book, *The Emperor's Babe* (2001), garnered significantly more attention.[209] She not only marketed her texts, but she also positioned herself within a globally networked literary field, with self-applications to the British Council's foreign literary tours programs, because she felt that she was being excluded from British-based literary festivals.[210] Even now, with a widely publicized three-book deal under her belt[211] post-Booker, Evaristo is not relying on the automatic dynamic that might bring to public attention her following works or those that preceded *Girl*,

---

[207] B. Evaristo, *Manifesto: On Never Giving Up* (London: Hamish Hamilton, 2021), p. 165.

[208] B. Evaristo, *Manifesto: On Never Giving Up* (London: Hamish Hamilton, 2021), p. 171.

[209] B. Evaristo, "The Stories We Tell," *Arvon* (October 1, 2019), www.arvon.org/bernardine-evaristo-the-stories-we-tell/.

[210] B. Evaristo, *Manifesto: On Never Giving Up* (London: Hamish Hamilton, 2021), p. 171.

[211] Cf. A. Chaves, "Booker Prize Winner Bernardine Evaristo Signs Three-Book Deal, Including New Memoir 'Manifesto'," *The National News* (March 27, 2021), www.thenationalnews.com/arts-culture/books/booker-prize-winner-bernardine-evaristo-signs-three-book-deal-including-new-memoir-manifesto-1.1192019. Interestingly, one of the books has been announced as her debut short story collection, a type of book which is usually unpopular with publishers. For context, see C. Norrick-Rühl, "Short Story Collections and Cycles in the British Literary Marketplace," in *Constructing Coherence in the British Short Story Cycle*, ed. P. Gill and F. Kläger (Houndsmills: Routledge, 2018), pp. 45–67.

Woman, Other. First launched at the Queen Elizabeth Hall, Southbank Centre on October 3, 2021, in conversation with Afua Hirsch, Evaristo has toured the United Kingdom to promote *Manifesto. On Never Giving Up* in a series of twelve in-person interviews.[212] Similarly, for the US rollout of the book in early 2022, Evaristo's publisher (Grove Atlantic, an independent publisher) planned a virtual tour across the continental USA, with a focus on independent bookstores as hosts.[213]

Summing up, then, it seems that Evaristo's understanding of economic success in the literary marketplace as trailblazing somewhat resonates with the positions and practices of other Black writers, and Toni Morrison would be a prominent example, though this is not always appreciated. White left-leaning academics have regularly signaled their skepticism of the extent to which market practice might facilitate empowerment.[214] Though there can be no doubt that BIPOC writers have faced multiple challenges and pressures to cater to marketized white expectations, we would like to stress that the inverse dynamic remains a *possibility*. Depending on an individual's practice and possibly leverage, commerce and culture do not have to be considered as binarily opposed; in some cases, apt navigation of publishing/commerce and indeed usage of its very own avenues and mechanisms ("publishers need to make money") can enable a diversification of given market conditions, not least because market systems themselves tend to rely on

---

[212] Cf. B. Evaristo (@BernardineEvari), "Looking forward to this & here you are on the tour poster now @SavidgeReads" [Twitter post, picture: Manifesto by Bernardine Evaristo Book Tour] (October 14, 2021), https://twitter.com/BernardineEvari/status/1448549154997874693.

[213] Grove Atlantic Books, Manifesto by Bernardine Evaristo: Author Tour Dates, https://groveatlantic.com/book/manifesto/.

[214] For example, Crosthwaite, in *The Market Logics of Contemporary Fiction*, is very hesitant about this possibility and rehearses the contested narrative of Toni Morrison's alleged sell-out to Oprah Winfrey (he writes of the "alliance between Morrison's canonical status and [Oprah] Winfrey's commercial power," p. 49).

the principle of innovation,[215] which also means avoiding such gatekeeping that hampers (marketable) progress.

As our previous reference to Steele's book already indicates, Evaristo's growing online presence and long-term apt internet usage for activist pursuits can be framed as hashtag activism and as such "a networked activity" and "counterpublic" approach "whereby individual tweets coalesce into a larger collective storytelling."[216] For sure, the wave of appreciation and urgency surrounding Black Lives Matter also contributed substantially to eventually raising Evaristo to the top of the Booker shortlist. Not only had Evaristo herself been a long-term advocate of the movement, her book and success also began trending under the Black Lives Matter hashtag. A week after the Booker announcement, Evaristo took to Twitter, her main social media go-to,[217] first thanking her editor Simon Prosser, with whom she has had a long and fruitful working relationship, and, second, her followers. ("Thank you for all your support on social media before and after the @TheBookerPrizes.") In her statement, the unwaning, long-term support of her (digital) fans and followers evoked a sense of consistent commitment – a long-established though growing network – that sharply contrasted with the rapidly increasing attention that the

---

[215] Cf. C. Koegler, *Critical Branding: Postcolonial Studies and the Market* (New York: Routledge, 2018), especially ch. 2: pp. 49–79, and ch. 4: pp. 105–116.

[216] S. J. Jackson, M. Bailey, and B. Foucault Welles, *#HashtagActivism: Networks of Race and Gender Justice* (Cambridge, MA: MIT Press, 2020), pp. 25, 24, 22.

[217] While Evaristo also uses Instagram, she tweets much more often than she posts on Instagram, and uses Twitter as a space for industry criticism and her activism much more clearly than on Instagram. At time of writing (February 2022), Evaristo had 36.5k followers on Instagram and posted every few days; at the same moment on Twitter, she had 69.4k followers and tweeted on a daily basis. For comparison, at time of revision (August 2022), Evaristo had 38.4k followers on Instagram and 74.0k followers on Twitter. Cf. B. Evaristo (@BernardineEvari) Twitter Profile, https://twitter.com/BernardineEvari and B. Evaristo (@bernardineevaristo) Instagram Profile, www.instagram.com/bernardineevaristo/.

Booker machinery now afforded and which propelled, not least, her followers from a couple of thousand to 69K+ now. She uses Twitter in ways that align with Michael Warner's analysis of public speech; her Twitter communication combines, in his words, "great urgency and intimate import";[218] this offers a particular sense of authenticity to readers and followers. In line with Black digital feminism's tendency for enthusiastic and occasionally cautionary notes on self-branding,[219] Evaristo has used Twitter in particular for her own ends that, as she readily admits, are not mutually exclusive with those of her publisher's commercial success; neither has she voiced any skepticism as to her and Atwood sharing the Booker, which was criticized by others as an only partial embrace of Evaristo's brilliant storytelling and heterodox position. In addition, since winning the Booker, Evaristo has actively leveraged her new status to powerfully further an agenda that is larger than her own. As aforementioned, she has launched her own book series within the Hamish Hamilton imprint at Penguin Random House. She has also continued to use her voice to lend support for initiatives such as *Re:Thinking Diversity*, the study we have quoted throughout this Element, and "Lit in Colour," a campaign to diversify school curricula.[220] These steps are logical, given her long-standing commitment to the diversification of the industry and industry-adjacent sectors, broadly understood. In a landmark decision, the Royal Society of Literature named Evaristo their next President – only the second woman writer in 200 years, and the first-ever writer of color.[221]

---

[218] M. Warner, *Publics and Counterpublics* (New York: Zone Books, 2002), p. 76.

[219] Cf. e.g., C. K. Steele, *Digital Black Feminism* (New York: New York University Press, 2021); F. Jones, *Reclaiming Our Space: How Black Feminism is Changing the World from the Tweets to the Streets* (Boston: Beacon Press, 2019).

[220] B. Evaristo, "A Diverse Curriculum Will Help Kids Grow Emotionally and Intellectually," *Penguin Articles* (June 29, 2021), www.penguin.co.uk/articles/ 2021/june/bernardine-evaristo-lit-in-colour-introduction.html.

[221] W. Caplan, "Bernardine Evaristo Has Been Named President of the Royal Society of Literature," *Literary Hub* (December 1, 2021), https://lithub.com/

While her ascent to the pinnacle of British literary culture has been widely acknowledged as overdue, there have been critical voices as well. True to her branding strategy, Evaristo has leveraged these critical voices to underline the biases prevalent in the media. In October 2021, cartoonist Kipper Williams, for instance, published a cartoon in which a radio listener, tuning in to BBC Radio 4, is exclaiming to his partner, "Quick! Bernardine Evaristo isn't on!," signaling the feeling that Evaristo has been granted too much media attention. Evaristo tweeted the cartoon, acknowledging that while she understood the humor, she had recently spent 2.5 hours on BBC Radio 4 out of 1,000s of broadcast hours per annum. In her tweet, she suggested the cartoon was indicative of the backlash Black women meet for "claiming a little space."[222]

The question of space also extends to the 2019 Booker prize. While the Booker was a windfall for Evaristo, it also bestowed visibility on the often biased workings of the attention economy and the literary field today, as we have already suggested in the Introduction (Section 1) to this Element. While, in her *Manifesto*, Evaristo describes her joint Booker win with Margaret Atwood as a "landmark historical moment for literature and for the sisterhood,"[223] reviewers were not as magnanimous. For instance, Justine Jordan in the *Guardian* called the decision a "fudge," saying: "To honour Evaristo's novel, which intertwines 12 narratives about black women in Britain, is to shine a much-deserved spotlight on an author who has blazed a trail in subject matter and style for a quarter of a century," commenting in passing that Atwood's book was "a huge event novel" and "global bestseller," "sprinkling some much-needed publishing

---

bernardine-evaristo-has-been-named-president-of-the-royal-society-of-litera ture/.

[222] B. Evaristo (@BernardineEvari), "If people object, is it because I'm a black woman claiming a little space?" [Twitter post] (October 31, 2021), https:// twitter.com/BernardineEvari/status/1454909915567427588.

[223] B. Evaristo, *Manifesto: On Never Giving Up* (London: Hamish Hamilton, 2021), p. 145.

glitz" as a much-anticipated sequel to *The Handmaid's Tale*.[224] Whether Evaristo finally received the attention and accolade she long deserved, or whether the committee's decision to have her share the prize with Atwood was actually scandalous, continues to be a matter of debate, though Evaristo herself has shown nothing but appreciation in the face of the events. Considering the range of awards and honorary positions she has received since, the Booker itself might have been crucial at the time, but retrospectively is one award of many honors she has since received, turning Evaristo into one of Britain's currently most influential writers.

Evaristo's online and offline advocacy continues to culminate in her book publications, which have a lasting impact on the industry and will certainly be canonized in the near future, if the works of other authors who have received prizes are any indication.[225] One final aspect that we would like to address here is gatekeeping, and the interesting fact that Evaristo clearly views her connection to editor Simon Prosser – a white male gatekeeper at a major conglomerate-owned publishing house – as central to her success, despite her otherwise countless activities and far-flung, often alternative networks. Evaristo emphasizes his role in her career repeatedly in interviews, on Twitter, as well as in her *Manifesto*. She has also commented on the central role of editors, such as that "we need the editors who will [...] help us craft our work. [...] You know, writers, we get so much attention, right? (Hopefully!) But actually, we wouldn't be doing what we're doing without the editors behind us."[226]

[224] J. Jordan, "Booker Judges Try to Have it Both Ways," *The Guardian* (October 14, 2019), www.theguardian.com/books/2019/oct/14/booker-judges-split-between-huge-event-novel-and-obscure-choice.

[225] For more context, see in particular this recent quantitative work: A. Manshel, L. B. McGrath, and J. D. Porter, "Who Cares about Literary Prizes?" *Public Books* (March 3, 2019), www.publicbooks.org/who-cares-about-literary-prizes/.

[226] Penguin Books UK, "Bernardine Evaristo and Her Editor on Their Working Relationship and Winning the Booker [Video]," *YouTube* (December 14, 2021), www.youtube.com/watch?v=qOtZblT_P0g.

Prosser has undoubtedly been a positive, formative influence on Evaristo's oeuvre – which speaks to the potentially productive aspects of gatekeeping in the sense of an alliance beyond the ties of discrimination and bias. Yet this relationship also needs to be seen in relation to a much larger system of gatekeeping that has had and still has the clear tendency to systematically disadvantage minority writers. We have tried to sketch this system out in the following way (Figure 1), seeking to show the multiple obstacles that writers face: from having the opportunity to write, and feeling that their voices matter, to multiple steps in between. As emerges, there are substantial gates to pass through which particularly call into question the oft-repeated meritocratic illusion that only the "best" books make it in the business (and "best" according to whom, anyway). Clearly, there are books that pass through these numerous gates with more ease than others, and usually (statistically speaking) they are the ones written by white, male authors.

We offer this sketch as a way of visualizing these obstacles and thinking them through, though this certainly is not a complete representation. As books pass through the gates, it is also important to keep in mind that, again, statistically speaking, the people who make the decisions are disproportionately white, male, cisgendered, heterosexual, and able-bodied, as studies such as the aforementioned Lee and Low Diversity Baseline Survey have illustrated. The gates, then, are still kept closed to a wide range of authors and texts. One could say that, instead of facilitating "difference" and diversity in the book world, the keys to the gates ultimately remain out of reach for many, implicitly or explicitly policing the boundaries of "difference." As we have intimated here, this is of course part of the reason why the digital literary sphere has thrived, and often in the sections of so-called minority authors or niche writing. To bring in Wattpad and similar platforms once more, it is not without reason that Black and LGBTQIA+ novels, as well as crossovers between the two (e.g., #BlackLGBTQ literature) draw large audiences there, some of the texts garnering millions of readers.

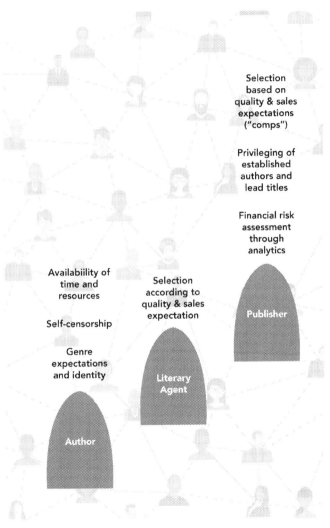

Figure 1 Gatekeeping in publishing. The successive "gates" represent the various stages of the publishing process, each of which presents its own set of obstacles to the writer

Reviewer/Critic

Trade Reviews

Reviews for journalistic output

Literary prize juries

New media reviews: podcasts, Bookstagram, Booktok, etc.

Bookseller

Selection based on trade reviews, quality & sales expectation

Choice of storefront displays

Reader

Familiarity with author/title

Means of access to books

Genre expectations

Peer group influence

Attention economy

CURATION IN THE BOOK INDUSTRY

Figure 1 (cont.)

5 Conclusion: The Book as Affect and the Novel as Network

Seventy years ago, the notion that "books are different" – a notion with ample historical precursors – was employed in a UK court setting where industry actors bartered for policy exemptions and a continuation of the Net Book Agreement. Even after the demise of the Net Book Agreement in 1997, however, the notion is perpetuated. This Element started out from the question "Are Books Still Different?" and has explored concepts of "difference" in the book trade and how difference might be understood in relation to literature as culture and commodity in an (increasingly) digital age. From a distinctly interdisciplinary perspective, interweaving book studies and literary studies, we have attempted to tease apart the concept of "difference": as a popular discourse within the industry and beyond, as a branding strategy, and as a focal point of cultural policy. On a metalevel, this interdisciplinary work has been very productive for us as writers, both fruitfully intertwining the commonalities between the two disciplines and illuminating relevant differences in method, research, writing styles, and traditions – these *differences* themselves emerging as instrumental in tackling the question of: "Are Books Still Different?"

Many of the points that we have touched upon beg a question that we have avoided thus far: What are books today, anyway? What does it mean to engage with books? While literary studies tend to focus on plot features and different possible readings as well as aesthetic and formal properties of books (which is where the preferred brand "literature" comes in), book studies offer models of thinking about the different roles that books potentially fulfill. In a wide-ranging and integrated perspective, Leslie Howsam, for example, differentiates between the book as a *text*, as a material *object*, as a cultural *transaction*, and as an *experience*.[227] Amaranth

---

[227] L. Howsam, "The Study of Book History," in *The Cambridge Companion to the History of the Book*, ed. L. Howsam (Cambridge: Cambridge University Press, 2015), pp. 1–13, here pp. 4–5, www.cambridge.org/core/books/cambridge-companion-to-the-history-of-the-book/study-of-book-history/048AF1E3C65E6 C742B5E962D96DE5B17.

Borsuk similarly offers four vantage points in her *The Book*: the book as *object*, the book as *content*, the book as *idea*, and the book as *interface*.[228] Tellingly, both authors offer distinct insights into the ways in which books are currently fetishized as objects, something that Jessica Pressman has termed "bookishness";[229] Borsuk prefers "bookness."[230] In any case, bookishness combines, unapologetically even, the cultural and commodified angle on literature that we have discussed and ultimately integrated in this Element. When visiting the Penguin Shop or the British Library Shop, one will encounter book jewelry, book Christmas tree ornaments, book paraphernalia for any walk of life from the beach to the boudoir (towels, scarves, bags, mugs, etc.). These products certainly play with (and on) the idea of books being "different" and "special," not least in the traditionally hard-copy format. Borsuk suggests that, "When the aesthetic of bookness itself is fetishized to such a degree that it can be bought and sold (as cell phone cases, home safes, and printed sportswear, for example), we've come full circle to the commodification of the book object."[231] What is more, this indicates a kind of cultural meta-textuality that not only becomes readable as text but also comes with its own aesthetic features and affective components. As Sydney Shep writes, books are "cultural metaphors" which "provoke affective experiences."[232] As such, while bookishness and corresponding marketing campaigns might be understood as post-digital or post-capitalist posturing, they do also signal Western culture's continuing, if not intensifying, sustained affective investment in the very idea of "the book." As we might therefore conclude, the book has

---

[228] Cf. A. Borsuk, *The Book* (Cambridge, MA: MIT Press, 2018).

[229] Cf. J. Pressman, *Bookishness: Loving Books in a Digital Age* (New York: Columbia University Press, 2020).

[230] A. Borsuk, *The Book* (Cambridge, MA: MIT Press, 2018), p. 113.

[231] A. Borsuk, *The Book* (Cambridge, MA: MIT Press, 2018), p. 113.

[232] S. Shep, "Books in Global Perspectives," in *The Cambridge Companion to the History of the Book*, ed. L. Howsam (Cambridge: Cambridge University Press, 2015), pp. 53–70, here p. 53, www.cambridge.org/core/books/abs/cambridge-companion-to-the-history-of-the-book/books-in-global-perspectives/A78179FA640E81F41B692E0DF4C16604.

become an affect – not overnight, but as the result of a long-standing process of conjoint valuation, branding, and mythification.

The-book-as-affect is intimately tied to the book's "different" or "special" nature that continues to excite and enthuse the masses, the branders, and the policymakers. The-book-as-affect presents a constant feedback loop to book discourse; it energizes a circuit of investment (financial; affective) and attention that is inextricably related with the branding of literature/books as culture and commodity in a digital age. It is also because of this that "literature" and "book" ultimately become collapsible into one another. Literature is sold in book form; it enters the public sphere in the form of books. At the same time, the aura of "literature" as well as individual periods, authors, texts, etc. directly informs – helps to energize, drive, code the meaning of – "the book." There is a constant, reciprocal feedback loop here, too. It is only because we can *narrate* the social meaning of books in particular ways that literature emerges as a valuable (read: "different") cultural good in fetishized book form, and vice versa. Affective currents, charging back and forth across the lines of discursive categorization, continue to permeate and blur the difference between the book and literature just as they blur the difference between literature as culture and commodity – particularly in a digital age.

Indeed, the-book-as-affect's reciprocal dynamics are only accelerated by recent digital technologies such as Instagram (subsumed under the #bookstagram hashtag) or TikTok (summarized as #BookTok). These dynamics hint at the enormous potential of digitally driven bookishness that all but abrogates the very differences between literature/the book as culture and literature/the book as commodity. Just as affective currents crisscross assumed forms of categorization and compartmentalization, in a similarly momentous development, #BookTok activities have been seen to drive younger consumers into brick-and-mortar bookshops in numbers not seen since the Harry Potter books were first published.[233] Thus, while we clearly

---

[233] Cf. S. Bayley, "BookTok Giving Bookshops a Boost Not Seen since Rowling, Says Daunt," *The Bookseller* (January 31, 2022), www.thebookseller.com/news/booktok-giving-bookshops-boost-not-seen-rowling-says-daunt-1302475?utm_source=Adestra.

can speak of a digital literary sphere, these developments indicate the extent to which that sphere ultimately remains interlinked with the physical modes of bookselling and distribution – just as the cultural status of literature/books remains intimately entangled with commoditization and, as one might add, self-branding with activism (and vice versa). Amazon's move towards brick-and-mortar locations, which raised concern in the traditional publishing industry, is another manifestation of such entanglement, though in early 2022 Amazon announced that they were closing all their brick-and-mortar locations.[234] Wherever the assumed signatory differences between literature as culture and commodity crumble; where the lines between traditional and digital publishing are redrawn, and where a post-capitalist bookishness reveals an affective investment in the book as a fetishized object that might have been with us for hundreds of years – in all these cases myriad outcomes arise to the advantage of different interest groups. These can redistribute authority and privilege just as much as profits, in various directions. Culture or commodity? Rather than a natural phenomenon, this difference is perhaps best understood as the long-term effect of normalized branding and valuation patterns – patterns that have produced the meaningfulness of such a difference in the first place (occasionally bordering on fetishism). The-book-as-affect is, as we might say, the commerce-positive, inverse mirror-function of branding books as "different," sneakily signaling the amount of labor and energy that goes into establishing the naturalness of the assumption of the book's "essential difference."

---

[234] For a critical analysis of Amazon's brick-and-mortar strategy and shortcomings thereof, see J. Tolentino, "Amazon's Brick-and-Mortar Stores Are Not Built For People Who Actually Read," *New Yorker* (May 30, 2017), www.newyorker .com/culture/cultural-comment/amazons-brick-and-mortar-bookstores-are-not-built-for-people-who-actually-read. On the recent closures, see K. Yee, "Good News Alert: Amazon is Closing its Physical Bookstores," *Literary Hub* (March 2, 2022), https://lithub.com/good-news-alert-amazon-is-closing-its-physical-bookstores/.

Throughout the course of this Element we have frequently taken recourse to the network approach, which we believe can help us frame and understand literature and its underlying circuits ranging from cultural to commercial. By focusing not only on the text itself but seeking to understand any text's connections to other textual forms, institutions, and actors in the novel network, we can gain a deeper understanding of the place(s) and platform(s) that literature inhabits today. There are, in our view, several advantages to the network approach. In regards to our title and question "Are Books Still Different?" the network approach firmly discounts the idea that books might be either: culture or commodity. Instead, as we have argued, the two are interconnected and rely on each other. Any book's appearance in what Judith Butler calls "the sphere of appearance,"[235] that is, any book that gains attention and traction does so because it has been marketed, promoted, branded, and so on, by those who wish to see it thrive – which includes gatekeepers of different kinds. Similarly, books are not naturally "different"; instead, we might prefer to *think* of them as different (or of literature as "singular") because of how "the book" and "literature" (sometimes with a capital L) are narrated and valorized. Indeed, in the book trade, *difference* has long been a brand narrative imbued with valorization. One could say that "books are different" itself is one of the oldest stories in the book – a self-perpetuating, self-fulfilling narrative (permeated by affective investment) that is continually driven by those who have stakes in the notion of books as different. As already indicated, this does not necessarily mean that we

---

[235] Butler writes: "Plural and public action is the exercise of the right to place and belonging, and this exercise is the means by which the space of appearance is presupposed and brought into being" (*Notes Toward a Performative Theory of Assembly* [Cambridge, MA: Harvard University Press, 2015], pp. 59–60, my emphasis). Broadening her concept, she moves on to speak of the "sphere of appearance" that we understand to incorporate the sum of all appearances that signal someone's or a group's effective claim to public visibility. Caroline Koegler works with several of Butler's concepts (the "sphere of appearance," performativity, materialisation, and others) in *Critical Branding: Postcolonial Studies and the Market* (New York: Routledge, 2018).

should abolish the notion of "difference" in relation to books or that it is wrong that "difference" is a brand; neither does bookishness equal a capitalist sellout. Instead, as we have suggested throughout, it might be important to rethink the premises and cornerstones upon which notions of difference are built in the first place. It is in further networking these (alleged) differences and their shared underpinnings that we might gain a deeper understanding of both culture and commodities in a digital age.

In rethinking "difference" in relation to literature/books, the network approach might encourage societies and their book industries to live up more fully to the brief of "bibliodiversity." Connections are necessary to establishing one's place in the literary sphere, and networks are central in gatekeeping processes. Networks not only give authors "permission to write," to quote again Evaristo's formative influences of Black female writers that she pulls together across the Atlantic as a young writer; networks can also, as we have seen, place authors in a position to be published and heard, blazing a trail for others. As such, any book that attains visibility in the public sphere – and the digital sphere increasingly plays a central part in this – potentially works like a promise, creating a space in which similar writers and stories might be heard. In this way, networks can open up new spaces and voices, and these, in turn, potentially give rise to new paths and networks, particularly if the social conditions are favorable. It is at these points that "networked counterpublics" or "diverse networks of dissent" (concepts that stem from research on internet activism), might be interlinked into more mainstream networks (as in Evaristo's case), by which orthodox circuits of valorization and attention might be changed. In turn, any such incorporation can of course also lead to forms of de-radicalization of activist practice and ideas which can ultimately harness heterodox movements – this, of course, is always the risk of absorption into the mainstream.

Given the limitations of the Element format, we have not been able to analyze in detail the changes wrought by self-publishing and platforms like Wattpad. Further research is needed to grasp these developments more fully, and – as they are "moving targets" – the research on them will have to be continuous and comparative in nature. Claire Parnell's forthcoming PhD research on Amazon and Wattpad and marginalized authors of romance points towards the potentials and challenges in this area.[236] As Layla Mohamed has also recently shown, there needs to be further discussion of the process of diversifying the industry; in her parsing, the industry needs to decolonize instead of diversify.[237] We hope that future research can profit from our observations on the network approach as well as on concepts of "difference" and diversity vis-à-vis literature as culture and (not or!) commodity in the digital age.

[236] Cf. C. Parnell, *Platform Publishing in the Entertainment Ecosystem: Experiences of Marginalised Authors on Amazon and Wattpad*, PhD project completion seminar, University of Melbourne (February 9, 2022).

[237] Qtd. in L. Mohamed, "Publishing Must Decolonise," *The Bookseller* (June 19, 2020), www.thebookseller.com/comment/publishing-must-decolonise-1207525.

6 Coda

Reading the proofs of our Element alongside nearly daily news about Elon Musk's changes to Twitter has prompted us to add this Coda to the manuscript. The situation at Twitter is driving home the malleability, and fragility, of the digital sphere at a new scale. While Twitter is not mentioned in these pages as the only social media platform with diversifying potentials, its function as part of the digital literary sphere cannot be underestimated. Twitter has been particularly conducive to the type of activism exhibited by Bernardine Evaristo and analyzed here. It is too soon to tell conclusively what will become of the platform, but it seems safe to say that the space has already irrevocably changed. Certainly, other platforms are in the wings. Most publishers have already been connecting with readers via Instagram. BookTok, which has mostly been a space inhabited by younger readers, might also find new popularity with an older demographic. Numerous major publishers, especially university presses, have established Mastodon accounts. For the foreseeable future, activities that were once centralized on Twitter might take on more networked forms across different platforms and outputs.

One takeaway from our Element, then, is that doing twenty-first-century book and literary studies means dealing with uncertainties. Our research focuses on moving targets, and this can generate interesting and surprising results. The printed word (when and if it is still printed) is deeply enmeshed within platforms, and susceptible to change in ways that it may not have been in the twentieth century. In light of this, and coming full circle, we are even more grateful for the platform that Cambridge Elements has offered us through its Publishing and Book Culture series. With a quick turnaround from submission to publication, though by nature still not quick enough to keep entirely apace with digital dynamics, we hope our Element will be read as a testament to what Ted Striphas has called "the late age of print".

Bibliography

Websites

Australian Society of Authors. Campaign: Parallel Importation. www
.asauthors.org/campaigns/parallel-importation.

Bernardine Evaristo Instagram Profile (@bernardineevaristo). www.instagram
.com/bernardineevaristo/.

Bernardine Evaristo Twitter Profile (@BerardineEvari). https://twitter
.com/BernardineEvari.

Grove Atlantic Books. Manifesto by Bernardine Evaristo: Author Tour
Dates. https://groveatlantic.com/book/manifesto/.

Hachette Book Group. https://vip7.hachette.co.uk/imprint/lbbg/
dialogue-books/page/little-brown-books/lbbg-imprint-dialogue/.

IPA Global Fixed Book Price Report 2014.www.internationalpublishers
.org/images/news/2014/global-fixed-price-report.pdf.

Legacy Lit.www.legacylitbooks.com/landing-page/meet-legacy-lit/.

Penguin. Black Britain: Writing Back Series.www.penguin.co.uk/series/
bbwb/black-britain—writing-back.html.

Penguin Books UK YouTube Channel.www.youtube.com/c/Penguin
BooksUK/about.

Publishizer. https://publishizer.com/.

The Booker Prize YouTube Channel (@TheBookerPrize). www.youtube
.com/channel/UCx0g6-WY4RMUBM9j2PmFusA.

The Booker Prizes. The 2019 Booker Prize.https://thebookerprizes.com/
the-booker-library/prize-years/2019.

The Stella Prize.https://thestellaprize.com.au/.

VIDA Women in Literary Arts.www.vidaweb.org/.

Sources and References

Ahnert, R., Ahnert, S. E., Coleman, C. N., and Weingart, S. B. (2020). *The Network Turn: Changing Perspectives in the Humanities*. Cambridge: Cambridge University Press. https://doi.org/10.1017/9781108866804.

Alcantara, J. (2019). The Diversity Baseline Survey. *Lee and Low Books*. www.leeandlow.com/about-us/the-diversity-baseline-survey.

Alter, A., and Harris, E. A. (2020). "There Are Tons of Brown Faces Missing": Publishers Step Up Diversity Efforts. *The New York Times*, October 29.

Bangert, J. (2019). *Buchhandelssystem und Wissensraum in der Frühen Neuzeit*. Berlin: De Gruyter Saur. https://doi.org/10.1515/9783110616521.

Baumbach, S. (2020). Marketing Anglophone World Literatures. In S. Helgesson, B. Neumann, and G. Rippl, eds., *Handbook of Anglophone World Literatures*. Berlin: De Gruyter, pp. 229–244.

Baverstock, A. (2019). Marketing for Publishing. In A. Phillips and M. Bhaskar, eds., *Oxford Handbook of Publishing*. Oxford: Oxford University Press, pp. 345–364. https://doi.org/10.1093/oxfordhb/9780198794202.013.15.

Baverstock, A., and Bowen, S. (2019). *How to Market Books*. New York: Routledge.

Bayley, S. (2022). BookTok Giving Bookshops a Boost Not Seen since Rowling, Says Daunt. *The Bookseller*, January 31. www.thebookseller.com/news/booktok-giving-bookshops-boost-not-seen-rowling-says-daunt-1302475?utm_source=Adestra.

Böker, E. (2018). *Skandinavische Bestseller auf dem deutschen Buchmarkt: Analyse des gegenwärtigen Literaturbooms*. Würzburg: Königshausen & Neumann.

Borsuk, A. (2018). *The Book*. Cambridge, MA: MIT Press.

Brouillette, S. (2011). *Postcolonial Writers and the Global Literary Marketplace*. London: Palgrave.

Brouillette, S. (2014). *Literature and the Creative Economy*. Redwood City: Stanford University Press.

Butler, J. (2015). *Notes Toward a Performative Theory of Assembly*. Cambridge, MA: Harvard University Press. https://doi.org/10.4159/9780674495548.

Caplan, W. (2021). Bernardine Evaristo Has Been Named President of the Royal Society of Literature. *Literary Hub*, December 1. https://lithub.com/bernardine-evaristo-has-been-named-president-of-the-royal-society-of-literature/.

Carlick, S. (2021). "Design Has the Power to Encourage People to Start Reading": Behind the Book Covers of Black Britain: Writing Back. *Penguin Random House*, February 5. www.penguin.co.uk/articles/2021/february/black-britain-writing-back-design-book-covers.html.

Carolan, S., and Evain, C. (2013). Self-Publishing: Opportunities and Threats in a New Age of Mass Culture. *Publishing Research Quarterly*, 29(4), 285–300. https://doi.org/10.1007/s12109-013-9326-3.

Casanova, P. (2007). *The World Republic of Letters*. Cambridge, MA: Harvard University Press.

Chaves, A. (2021). Booker Prize Winner Bernardine Evaristo Signs Three-Book Deal, Including New Memoir "Manifesto." *The National News*, March 27. www.thenationalnews.com/arts-culture/books/booker-prize-winner-bernardine-evaristo-signs-three-book-deal-including-new-memoir-manifesto-1.1192019.

Clark, J. Prommer, E., George, N. et al. (2019). The Lack of Visibility of Female Authors in the Media: Result of the Long-Term Research Project #countingwomen of the Cross-Association AG DIVERSITÄT of Literature Business and the Department for Media Research at University Rostock. Website: Frauenzählen.de.

The_Lack_of_Visibility_of_Female_Authors_in_the_Media_Results_of_a_Quantitative_Survey.pdf (xn--frauenzhlen-r8a.de).

Crosthwaite, P. (2019). *The Market Logics of Contemporary Fiction*. Cambridge: Cambridge University Press.

Curtain, J. (1993). Takeovers, Entertainment, Information & the Book. *Media Information Australia*, 68(1), 43–48. https://doi.org/10.1177/1329878X9306800108.

Davis, M. (2021). The Online Anti-public Sphere. *European Journal of Cultural Studies*, 24(1), 143–159. https://doi.org/10.1177/1367549420902799.

de León, C., Alter, A., Harris, E. A., and Khatib, J. (2020). "A Conflicted Cultural Force": What It's Like to Be Black in Publishing. *The New York Times*, July 1; updated June 3, 2021. www.nytimes.com/2020/07/01/books/book-publishing-black.html?action=click&module=RelatedLinks&pgtype=Article.

de León, C., and Harris, E. A. (2020). #PublishingPaidMe and a Day of Action Reveal an Industry Reckoning. *The New York Times*, June 10. www.nytimes.com/2020/06/08/books/publishingpaidme-publishing-day-of-action.html.

Dearnley, J. and Feather, J., (2002). The UK Bookselling Trade without Resale Price Maintenance – An Overview of Change 1995–2001. *Publishing Research Quarterly*, 17, 16–31.

Deutsche Monopolkommision. (2018). Fixed Book Prizes in a Changing Market Environment. Special Report No. 80. www.monopolkommission.de/images/PDF/SG/s80_fulltext.pdf.

Deutscher Bundestag. (2018). Antrag der Fraktionen der CDU/CSU und SPD "Kulturgut Buch fördern – Buchpreisbindung erhalten." Drucksache 19/6413. https://dserver.bundestag.de/btd/19/064/1906413.pdf.

Driscoll, B., and Squires, C. (2020). Megativity and Miniaturization at the Frankfurt Book Fair. *Post45*, August 4. https://post45.org/2020/04/megativity-and-miniaturization-at-the-frankfurt-book-fair/.

Duvezin-Caubet, C. (2020). Gaily Ever After: Neo-Victorian M/M Genre Romance for the Twenty-First Century. *Neo-Victorian Studies*, 13(1), 246–247. https://doi.org/10.5281/zenodo.4320839.

English, J. F. (2005). *The Economy of Prestige: Prizes, Awards, and the Circulation of Cultural Value*. Cambridge, MA: Harvard University Press.

Evaristo, B. (2019). The Stories We Tell. *Arvon*, October 1. www.arvon .org/bernardine-evaristo-the-stories-we-tell/.

Evaristo, B. (2019). (@BernardineEvari) "Pls RT: The @BBC described me yesterday as 'another author' apropos @TheBookerPrizes 2019. How quickly & casually they have removed my name from history." *Twitter*, December 4. https://twitter.com/BernardineEvari/status/ 1202103687231016960.

Evaristo, B. (2021). A Diverse Curriculum Will Help Kids Grow Emotionally and Intellectually. *Penguin Articles*, June 29. www.penguin .co.uk/articles/2021/june/bernardine-evaristo-lit-in-colour-introduc tion.html.

Evaristo, B. (2021). *Manifesto. On Never Giving Up*. London: Hamish Hamilton.

Evaristo, B. (2021). (@BernardineEvari) "If People object, is it because I'm a black woman claiming a little space?" *Twitter*, October 31. https:// twitter.com/BernardineEvari/status/1454909915567427588.

Evaristo, B. (2021). (@BernardineEvari) "Looking forward to this & here you are on the tour poster now @SavidgeReads [Picture: Manifesto by Bernardine Evaristo Book Tour]." *Twitter*, October 14. https://twitter .com/BernardineEvari/status/1448549154997874693.

Everett, A. (2002). The Revolution Will Be Digitized: Afrocenticity and the Digital Public Sphere. *Social Text*, 20(2), 125–146. https://muse.jhu .edu/article/31928.

Finkelstein, D., and McCleery, A. (2012). *Introduction to Book History*. London: Routledge.

Flood, A. (2019). "Another Author": Outrage after BBC Elides Bernardine Evaristo's Booker Win. *The Guardian*, December 4. www.theguardian .com/books/2019/dec/04/another-author-outrage-after-bbc-elides-bernardine-evaristo-booker-win.

Flood, A. (2019). Bernardine Evaristo Doubles Lifetime Sales in Five Days after Joint Booker Win. *The Guardian*, October 22. www.theguardian .com/books/2019/oct/22/bernardine-evaristo-doubles-lifetime-sales-in-five-days-after-joint-booker-win.

Flood, A. (2020). England's Bookshops Should Be Classed as Essential, Booksellers Argue. *The Guardian*, November 10. https://amp.the guardian.com/books/2020/nov/10/englands-bookshops-should-be-classed-as-essential-booksellers-argue?__twitter_impression= true.

Flood, A. (2020). French Bookshops Ask to Be Treated as Essential Services during New Lockdown. *The Guardian*, October 29. www .theguardian.com/books/2020/oct/29/french-bookshops-ask-to-be-treated-as-essential-services-during-new-lockdown.

Flood, A. (2020). #Publishingpaidme: Authors Share Advances to Expose Racial Disparities. *The Guardian*, June 8. www.theguardian.com/ books/2020/jun/08/publishingpaidme-authors-share-advances-to-expose-racial-disparities.

Gilroy, B. (2021). *Black Teacher*. London: Faber & Faber, Kindle ed.

Gottschalk, K. (2021). Comedy-Autorin über Aktivismus: "Twitter ist für mich Battle-Rap." *taz*, October 23. https://taz.de/Comedy-Autorin-ueber-Aktivismus/!5807195/.

Guernsey, L., Prescott, S., and Park, C. (February 25, 2021). Public Libraries and the Pandemic. *New America*. https://files.eric.ed.gov/full text/ED612400.pdf.

Halberstam, J. (2011). *The Queer Art of Failure*. Durham: Duke University Press.

Harris, E. A. (2021). In Backlash to Racial Reckoning, Conservative Publishers See Gold. *The New York Times*, August 15. www.nytimes.com/2021/08/15/books/race-antiracism-publishing.html.

Hawthorne, S. (2014). *Bibliodiversity: A Manifesto for Independent Publishing*. North Geelong: Spinifex Press.

Hernandez, D. (2020). "American Dirt" Was Supposed to Be a Publishing Triumph: What Went Wrong? *Los Angeles Times*, January 26. www.latimes.com/entertainment-arts/story/2020-01-26/american-dirt-publishing-latino-representation.

Hertwig, L. (2022). Bibliodiversität im Kontext des französischen Ehrengastauftritts *Francfort en français* auf der Frankfurter Buchmesse 2017: Die ganze Vielfalt des Publizierens in französischer Sprache? Unpublished PhD dissertation, University of Flensburg.

Howsam, L. (2015). The Study of Book History. In L. Howsam, ed., *The Cambridge Companion to the History of the Book*. Cambridge: Cambridge University Press, pp. 1–13. www.cambridge.org/core/books/cambridge-companion-to-the-history-of-the-book/study-of-book-history/048AF1E3C65E6C742B5E962D96DE5B17.

Huggan, G. (1997). Prizing "Otherness": A Short History of the Booker. *Studies in the Novel*, 29(3), 412–433. www.jstor.org/stable/29533224.

Huggan, G. (2001). *The Postcolonial Exotic: Marketing the Margins*. London: Routledge.

Huggan, G. (2020). Re-evaluating the Postcolonial Exotic. *Interventions: International Journal of Postcolonial Studies*, 22(7), 808–824. https://doi.org/10.1080/1369801X.2020.1753552.

International Publishers Association. (2014). Global Fixed Book Price Report. May 23. www.internationalpublishers.org/images/news/2014/global-fixed-price-report.pdf.

International Publishers Association and Federation of European Publishers. (2018). VAT on Books: The IPA-FEP Annual Global

Report 2018. https://internationalpublishers.org/images/aa-content/news/news-2019/IPA_ANNUAL_GLOBAL_REPORT_2018_2.pdf.

Jackson, S. J., Bailey, M., and Foucault Welles, B. (2020). *#HashtagActivism: Networks of Race and Gender Justice*. Cambridge, MA: MIT Press.

Jackson, S. J., and Foucault Welles, B. (2015). Hijacking #myNYPD: Social Media Dissent and Networked Counterpublics. *Journal of Communication*, 65(6), 932–952. https://doi.org/10.1111/jcom.12185.

Jeannotte, M. S. (2021). When the Gigs Are Gone: Valuing Arts, Culture and Media in the COVID-19 Pandemic. *Social Sciences & Humanities Open*, 3(1), 100097, pp. 1–7. https://doi.org/10.1016/j.ssaho.2020.100097.

Jones, F. (2019). *Reclaiming Our Space: How Black Feminism is Changing the World from the Tweets to the Streets*. Boston: Beacon Press.

Jordan, J. (2019). Booker Judges Try to Have it Both Ways. *The Guardian*, October 14. www.theguardian.com/books/2019/oct/14/booker-judges-split-between-huge-event-novel-and-obscure-choice.

Jordison, S. (2019). What Happened? *TLS*, October 25. www.the-tls.co.uk/articles/what-happened-booker-prize-ellmann/.

Josephs, K. B., and Risam, R. (2021). Introduction: The Digital Black Atlantic. In R. Risam and K. B. Josephs, eds., *The Digital Black Atlantic*. Minneapolis: University of Minnesota Press, pp. ix–xxiv. https://doi.org/10.5749/j.ctv1kchp41.3.

Keene, J. (2015). The Work of Black Literature in the Age of Digital Reproducibility. *Obsidian*, 41(1/2), 288–315. www.jstor.org/stable/44489472.

Kilkenny, K. (2018). Margaret Atwood Says Bulk of Hulu "Handmaid's Tale" Profits Went to MGM. *The Hollywood Reporter*, February 2. www.hollywoodreporter.com/tv/tv-news/margaret-atwood-says-bulk-hulu-handmaids-tale-profits-went-mgm-1081423/.

Kinder, K. (2021). *The Radical Bookstore: Counterspace for Social Movements*. Minneapolis: University of Minnesota Press.

Kirschenbaum, M. G. (2021). *Bitstreams: The Future of Digital Literary Heritage*. Philadelphia: University of Pennsylvania Press.

Koegler, C. (2018). *Critical Branding: Postcolonial Studies and the Market*. New York: Routledge.

Koegler, C. (2021). Uneasy Forms of Interdisciplinarity: Literature, Business Studies, and the Limits of Critique. *Anglistik: International Journal of English Studies*, 32(3), 33–51. https://doi.org/10.33675/ANGL/2021/3/6.

Koegler, C. (2022). Memorialising African Being and Becoming in the Atlantic World: Affective Her-Stories by Yaa Gyasi and Bernardine Evaristo. In T. W. Reeser, ed., *The Routledge Companion to Gender and Affect*. New York: Routledge, pp. 374–385.

Koegler, C., Norrick-Rühl, C., Pohlmann, P., and Sieg, G. (2023, forthcoming). "Must Writers Be Moral?": Interdisziplinäre Perspektiven auf "Morality Clauses." In E. Achermann, A. Blödorn, P. Pohlmann, and C. Norrick-Rühl, eds., *Literatur und Recht: Materialität: Formen und Prozesse gegenseitiger Vergegenständlichung*. Berlin: De Gruyter.

Kurschus, S. (2014). *European Book Cultures: Diversity as a Challenge*. Wiesbaden: Springer VS. https://doi.org/10.1007/978-3-658-08060-0.

Lähdesmäki, T., Koistinen, A. K., and Ylönen, S. C. (2020). Affective Rhetoric and "Sticky Concepts" in European Education Policy Documents. In *Intercultural Dialogue in the European Education Policies*. Cham: Palgrave Macmillan, pp. 81–98. https://doi.org/10.1007/978-3-030-41517-4_5.

Lee, E. (2004). *No Future: Queer Theory and the Death Drive*. Durham: Duke University Press.

Leetsch, J. (2022). From Instagram Poetry to Autofictional Memoir and Back Again: Experimental Black Life Writing in Yrsa Daley-Ward's Work. *Tulsa Studies in Women's Literature*, 41(2), 301–326.

Leypoldt, G. (2014). Singularity and the Literary Market. *New Literary History*, 45(1), 71–88.

Liu, R. (2020). How Bernardine Evaristo Won the Booker. *Prospect*, May 2. www.prospectmagazine.co.uk/magazine/bernardine-evaristo-girl-woman-other-interview-profile.

Mactavish, K. (2022). Crisis Book Browsing: Restructuring the Retail Shelf Life of Books. In C. Norrick-Rühl and S. Towheed, eds., *Bookshelves in the Age of the COVID-19 Pandemic*. London: Palgrave, pp. 49–68.

Mansfield, K. (2019). Record-Breaking US Sales for the Testaments. *The Bookseller*, September 16. www.thebookseller.com/news/record-breaking-us-sales-testaments-1081431.

Manshel, A., McGrath, L. B., and Porter, J. D. (2019). Who Cares about Literary Prizes? *Public Books*, March 3. www.publicbooks.org/who-cares-about-literary-prizes/.

Marsden, S. (2018). Why I'm Done with the Man Booker Prize and You Should Be too. *Medium*, July 10. https://medium.com/@steviemarsden/why-im-done-with-the-man-booker-prize-and-you-should-be-too-ad0057b95baf.

Marsden, S. (2021). *Prizing Scottish Literature: A Cultural History of the Saltire Society Literary Awards*. Cambridge: Cambridge University Press.

Matting, M. (2020). Warum eine exklusive Bindung an Amazon via KDP select gut für den Autor ist – und warum nicht. *Die Self-Publisher-Bibel*, November 17. www.selfpublisherbibel.de/warum-eine-exklusive-bindung-an-amazon-gut-fur-den-autor-ist-und-warum-nicht/.

McGrath, L. (2019). Comping White. *Los Angeles Review of Books*, January 19. https://lareviewofbooks.org/article/comping-white/.

Miller, L. J. (2006). *Reluctant Capitalists: Bookselling and the Culture of Consumption*. Chicago: University of Chicago Press.

Mohamed, L. (2020). Publishing Must Decolonise. *The Bookseller*, June 19. www.thebookseller.com/comment/publishing-must-decolonise-1207525.

Mohdin, A., Thomas, T., Quach, G., and Šeško, Z. (2021). One in Five Shortlisted Authors for Top UK Literary Prizes in 2020 were Black. *The Guardian*, October 1. www.theguardian.com/world/2021/oct/01/shortlisted-authors-uk-literary-prizes-black-diversity.

Moseley, M. (2022). *A History of the Booker Prize: Contemporary Fiction since 1992.* New York: Routledge.

Murray, S. (2012). *The Adaptation Industry: The Cultural Economy of Contemporary Literary Adaptation.* New York: Routledge.

Murray, S. (2018). *The Digital Literary Sphere: Reading, Writing, and Selling Books in the Internet Era.* Baltimore: Johns Hopkins University Press.

Murray, S. (2020). 10 Myths about Digital Literary Culture. *Post45*, August 4. https://post45.org/2020/04/10-myths-about-digital-literary-culture/.

Murray, S. (2021). Secret Agents: Algorithmic Culture, Goodreads and Datafication of the Contemporary Book World. *European Journal of Cultural Studies*, 24(4), 970–989. https://doi.org/10.1177/1367549419886026.

Nawotka, E. (2020). European E-book, Audiobook Sales See Pandemic Pop. *Publishers Weekly*, August 13. www.publishersweekly.com/pw/by-topic/international/international-book-news/article/84080-european-e-book-audiobook-sales-see-pandemic-pop.html.

Noble, S. U. (2018). *Algorithms of Oppression: How Search Engines Reinforce Racism.* New York: New York University Press.

Noorda, R. (2021). *Entrepreneurial Identity in US Book Publishing in the Twenty-First Century.* Cambridge: Cambridge University Press. www.cambridge.org/core/elements/entrepreneurial-identity-in-us-book-

publishing-in-the-twentyfirst-century/BA08F39C6C448AB1544D292E
61F2B85A.

Norrick-Rühl, C. (2018). Short Story Collections and Cycles in the British
Literary Marketplace. In P. Gill and F. Kläger, eds., *Constructing
Coherence in the British Short Story Cycle*. Houndsmills: Routledge, pp.
45–67.

Norrick-Rühl, C. (2019). *Internationaler Buchmarkt*. Frankfurt: Bramann.

Norrick-Rühl, C. (2022). Elmer the Elephant in the Zoom Room?
Reflections on Parenting, Book Accessibility and Screen Time in
a Pandemic. In C. Norrick-Rühl and S. Towheed, eds., *Bookshelves in
the Age of the COVID-19 Pandemic*. London: Palgrave, pp. 195–214.

Norrick-Rühl, C. (2023, forthcoming). Politics at Play in the Kabuff: The
Buchmesse as a Political Space. In B. Driscoll and C. Squires, eds., *The
Frankfurt Kabuff Critical Edition*.

Lanzendörfer, T., and Norrick-Rühl, C. (2020). *The Novel as Network:
Forms, Ideas, Commodities*. London: Palgrave Macmillan. https://doi
.org/10.1007/978-3-030-53409-7.

Norrick-Rühl, C., and Towheed, S. (2022). Introduction. In C. Norrick-
Rühl and S. Towheed, eds., *Bookshelves in the Age of the COVID-19
Pandemic*. London: Palgrave, pp.1–27.

Parnell, C. (2022). Platform Publishing in the Entertainment Ecosystem:
Experiences of Marginalised Authors on Amazon and Wattpad. PhD
project completion seminar, University of Melbourne.

Penguin Articles. (2020). Bernardine Evaristo Rediscovers Six Novels by
Black Writers for Black Britain: Writing Back Series. October 28. www
.penguin.co.uk/articles/2020/october/black-britain-writing-back-
bernardine-evaristo-hamish-hamilton-series.html.

Penguin Books UK. (2021). Bernardine Evaristo and Her Editor on Their
Working Relationship and Winning the Booker [Video]. *YouTube*,
December 14. www.youtube.com/watch?v=qOtZblT_P0 g.

Penguin Random House. (2019). Behind the Book: Inside Vintage's Publicity Campaign for the Testaments. December 12. www.penguin .co.uk/articles/company/blogs/behind-the-book–inside-vintage-s-campaign-for-margaret-atwood-s.html.

Peter, C. A. (2022). *Kulturgut Buch: Die Legitimation des Kartellrechtlichen Preisbindungsprivilegs von Büchern – Schutzzweck, Schutzgegenstand und Wirkungen des Buchpreisbindungsgesetzes*. Berlin: Springer.

Peterson, A. (2020). Bernardine Evaristo's Novels Get a Makeover. *Brittle Paper*, April 13. https://brittlepaper.com/2020/04/bernardine-evaristos-novels-get-a-makeover/.

Phillips, A., and Bhaskar, M., eds. (2019). *Oxford Handbook of Publishing*. Oxford: Oxford University Press.

Ponzanesi, S. (2014). *The Postcolonial Cultural Industry: Icons, Markets, Mythologies*. London: Palgrave.

Poort, J., and van Eijk, N. (2017). Digital Fixation: The Law and Economics of a Fixed E-book Price. *International Journal of Cultural Policy*, 23(4), 464–481. https://doi.org/10.1080/10286632.2015.1061516.

Pressman, J. (2020). *Bookishness: Loving Books in a Digital Age*. New York: Columbia University Press.

Publishers Weekly. (2020). Publishers Weekly Launches #BooksAre-Essential – Hashtag Campaign to Support Publishing Industry in Face of Covid-19. April 20. www.publishersweekly.com/pw/corp/BooksAre EssentialPressRelease.html.

Ramdarshan Bold, M. (2018). The Return of the Social Author. *Convergence: The International Journal of Research into New Media Technologies*, 24(2), 117–136. https://journals.sagepub.com/doi/abs/ 10.1177/1354856516654459.

Ramdarshan Bold, M., and Norrick-Rühl, C. (2017). The Independent Foreign Fiction Prize and Man Booker International Prize Merger. *Logos*, 28(3), 7–24. https://doi.org/10.1163/1878-4712-11112131.

Ramone, J. (2020). *Postcolonial Literatures in the Local Literary Marketplace*. London: Palgrave Macmillan, Kindle ed.

Ray Murray, P. (2019). The Digital Book. In A. Nash, C. Squires, and I. R. Willison, eds., *The Cambridge History of the Book in Britain. Vol. 7: The Twentieth Century and Beyond*. Cambridge: Cambridge University Press, 85–96.

Read, P. F. (2015). On Culture and Commerce: A Comparison of Government Support for Book Publishing in Canada, France, Germany and the United Kingdom. Inaugural dissertation published online on the JGU server. https://openscience.ub.uni-mainz.de/bit stream/20.500.12030/4045/1/100000508.pdf.

Reid, C. (2020). Amistad Launches #BlackoutBestsellerList on Social Media. *Publishers Weekly*, June 15. www.publishersweekly.com/pw/by-topic/industry-news/publisher-news/article/83593-amistad-launches-blackoutbestsellerlist-on-social-media.html.

Rekdal, P. (2021). *Appropriate: A Provocation*. New York: WW Norton.

Ribarovska, A. K., Hutchinson, M. R., Pittman, Q. J., Pariante, C., and Spencer, S. J. (2021). Gender Inequality in Publishing during the COVID-19 Pandemic. *Brain Behavior, and Immunity*, 91, 1–3. https://doi.org/10.1016/j.bbi.2020.11.022.

Risam, R., and Josephs, K. B. (2021). *The Digital Black Atlantic*. Minneapolis: University of Minnesota Press.

Rosen, J. (2021). Another Pandemic Surprise: A Mini Indie Bookstore Boom. *Publishers Weekly*, October 15. www.publishersweekly.com/pw/by-topic/industry-news/bookselling/article/87648-another-pandemic-surprise-a-mini-indie-bookstore-boom.html.

Russell, A. (2022). How Bernardine Evaristo Conquered British Literature. *The New Yorker*, February 3. www.newyorker.com/culture/persons-of-interest/how-bernardine-evaristo-conquered-british-literature.

Saha, A. (2016). The Rationalizing/Racializing Logic of Capital in Cultural Production. *Media Industries*, 3(1), 1–16. https://doi.org/10.3998/mij.15031809.0003.101.

Saha, A. (2021). *Race, Culture and Media*. London: Sage, Kindle ed.

Saha, A., and van Lente, S. (2020). *RE:Thinking "Diversity" in Publishing*. London: Goldsmith Press. www.spreadtheword.org.uk/wp-content/uploads/2020/06/Rethinking_diversity_in-publishing_WEB.pdf.

Saha, A., and van Lente, S. (2022). Diversity, Media and Racial Capitalism: A Case Study on Publishing. *Racial and Ethnic Studies*, 45(16), 216–236. https://doi.org/10.1080/01419870.2022.2032250.

Sánchez Prado, I. M. (2021). Commodifying Mexico: On *American Dirt* and the Cultural Politics of a Manufactured Bestseller. *American Literary History*, 33(2), 371–393. https://doi.org/10.1093/alh/ajab039.

Sapiro, G. (2016). How Do Literary Works Cross Borders (or Not)? A Sociological Approach to World Literature. *Journal of World Literature*, 1, 81–96. https://doi.org/10.1163/24056480-00101009.

Schivone, G. M. (2019). Corporate Censorship Is a Serious, and Mostly Invisible Threat to Publishing. *Electric Literature*, January 17. https://electricliterature.com/corporate-censorship-is-a-serious-and-mostly-invisible-threat-to-publishing/.

Schober, R. (2019). Adaptation as Connection: A Network Theoretical Approach to Convergence, Participation, and Co-production. In J. Fehrle and W. Schäfke, eds., *Adaptation in the Age of Media Convergence*. Amsterdam: Amsterdam University Press, pp. 31–56. https://doi.org/10.1515/9789048534012-002.

Sehgal, P. (2021). All You Can Read: Is Amazon Changing the Novel? *The New Yorker*, November 1, pp. 75–78. www.newyorker.com/magazine/2021/11/01/is-amazon-changing-the-novel-everything-and-less.

Seifert, N. (2021). *Frauen Literatur: Abgewertet, vergessen, wiederentdeckt*. Cologne: Kiepenheuer & Witsch.

Semuels, A. (2018). The Authors Who Love Amazon. *The Atlantic*, July 20. www.theatlantic.com/technology/archive/2018/07/amazon-kindle-unlimited-self-publishing/565664/.

Senft, T., and Noble, S. (2013). Race and Social Media. In J. Hunsinger and T. Senft, eds., *The Social Media Handbook*. New York: Routledge, pp. 107–125.

Shapiro, L. (2021). Blurbed to Death: How One of Publishing's Most Hyped Books Became its Biggest Horror Story – and Still Ended Up a Best Seller. *Vulture*, January 5. www.vulture.com/article/american-dirt-jeanine-cummins-book-controversy.html.

Sheehan, D. (2021). Sally Rooney's New Novel is Now the Most Reviewed Book of All Time. *Literary Hub*, September 17. https://lithub.com/sally-rooneys-new-novel-is-now-the-most-reviewed-book-of-all-time/.

Shep, S. (2015). Books in Global Perspectives. In L. Howsam, ed., *The Cambridge Companion to the History of the Book*. Cambridge: Cambridge University Press, pp. 53–70. www.cambridge.org/core/books/abs/cambridge-companion-to-the-history-of-the-book/books-in-global-perspectives/A78179FA640E81F41B692E0DF4C16604.

Sinykin, D. (2022). Millennial Fiction and the Question of Generations. Paper held at MLA 2022. www.dansinykin.com/mla-2022.

Skains, R. L. (2019). *Digital Authorship: Publishing in the Attention Economy*. Cambridge: Cambridge University Press. www.cambridge.org/core/elements/abs/digital-authorship/C47B1D69263C882BFFC20DFD9F290F38.

So, R. J. (2020). *Redlining Culture: A Data History of Racial Inequality and Postwar Fiction*. New York: Columbia University Press.

So, R. J., and Wezerek, G. (2020). Just How White Is the Book Industry? *The New York Times*, December 11. www.nytimes.com/interactive/2020/12/11/opinion/culture/diversity-publishing-industry.html.

Squires, C. (2007). *Marketing Literature: The Making of Contemporary Writing in Britain*. London: Palgrave Macmillan.

Squires, C. (2013). Literary Prizes and Awards. In G. Harper, ed., *A Companion to Creative Writing*. London: John Wiley, pp. 291–302.

Squires, C. (2020). Essential? Different? Exceptional? The Book Trade and Covid-19. *C21 Literature*, posted by K. Shaw, December 10. https://c21 .openlibhums.org/news/403/.

Steele, C. K. (2017). Black Bloggers and Their Varied Publics: The Everyday Politics of Black Discourse Online. *Television and New Media*, 19(2), 112–127. https://doi.org/10.1177/1527476417709535.

Steele, C. K. (2021). *Digital Black Feminism*. New York: New York University Press.

Steiner, A. (2017). Select, Display, and Sell: Curation Practices in the Bookshop. *Logos*, 28(4), 18–31. https://doi.org/10.1163/1878-4712-11112138.

Steiner, A. (2018). The Global Book: Micropublishing, Conglomerate Production, and Digital Market Structures. *Publishing Research Quarterly*, 34, 118–132. https://link.springer.com/article/10.1007/s12109-017-9558-8.

Stevenson, I. (2010). *Book Makers: British Publishing in the Twentieth Century*. London: The British Library Publishing Division,

Stevenson, I. (2019). Distribution and Bookselling. In A. Nash, C. Squires, and I. Willison, eds., *The Cambridge History of the Book in Britain. Vol. 7: The Twentieth Century and Beyond*. Cambridge: Cambridge University Press, pp. 191–230. www.cambridge.org/core/books/cambridge-history-of-the-book-in-britain/distribution-and-bookselling/3FB119A6 4003691769816D5EC4B91979#CN-bp-6.

Striphas, T. (2009). *The Late Age of Print: Everyday Book Culture from Consumerism to Control*. New York: Columbia University Press.

Sweney, M. (2020). Pandemic Drives Ebook and Audiobook Sales by UK Publishers to All-Time High. *The Guardian*, November 14. www.the

guardian.com/books/2020/nov/14/pandemic-drives-ebook-and-audio
book-sales-by-uk-publishers-to-all-time-high-covid.

Tepper, A. (2019). The Little Book That Could: How Bernardine Evaristo
Became an International Writer-to-Watch in 2019. *Vanity Fair*,
December 13. www.vanityfair.com/style/2019/12/bernardine-evaristo-
girl-woman-other-interview.

TheBookerPrizes. Youtube Channel. www.youtube.com/c/TheBooker
Prizes/about.

TheBookerPrizes. (2019). 2019 Booker Prize Shortlist Author Video –
Bernardine Evaristo [Video]. *YouTube*, October 14. www.youtube
.com/watch?v=jb7j-ZoUN4M&list=PLf5wOwLcmpzmF-7Bdeaw13e8k
ToXD7Uoq&index=4.

TheBookerPrizes. (2019). 2019 Booker Prize Shortlist Author Video –
Margaret Atwood [Video]. *YouTube*, October 16. www.youtube.com/
watch?v=4iLY9TExq2Q&list=PLf5wOwLcmpzmF-7Bdeaw13e8k
ToXD7Uoq&index=8.

TheBookerPrizes. (2019). The 2019 Booker Prize Longlist Announced
[Video]. *YouTube*, July 24. www.youtube.com/watch?v=9DS17Q1zf64
&list=PLf5wOwLcmpzmF-7Bdeaw13e8kToXD7Uoq&index=1.

TheBookerPrizes. (2019). The 2019 Booker Prize Winner Announced
[Video]. *YouTube*, October 14. www.youtube.com/watch?v=bgGTJg
IO0Uc&list=PLf5wOwLcmpzmF-7Bdeaw13e8kToXD7Uoq&
index=10.

TheBookerPrizes. (2020). The 2020 Booker Prize Longlist Announcement
[Video]. *YouTube*, July 28. www.youtube.com/watch?v=AYbYLL7lLbM.

TheBookerPrizes. (2021). 2021 Booker Prize Longlist Announced [Video].
YouTube, July 27. www.youtube.com/watch?v=PIrKprfwhJ
M&list=PLf5wOwLcmpzl_vatzqC3p4lKiwsG3d4zv&index=33.

Thompson, J. B. (2012). *Merchants of Culture: The Publishing Business in the
Twenty-First Century*. London: Plume.

Thompson, J. B. (2021). *Book Wars: The Digital Revolution in Publishing*. London: Polity Press.

Tolentino, J. (2017). Amazon's Brick-and-Mortar Stores Are Not Built For People Who Actually Read. *The New Yorker*, May 30. www.newyorker .com/culture/cultural-comment/amazons-brick-and-mortar-book stores-are-not-built-for-people-who-actually-read.

Wabuke, H. (2022). "Manifesto" is a Story of Dreams Made Real by Never Giving Up. *NPR*, January 18. www.npr.org/2022/01/18/1073739054/ manifesto-is-a-story-of-dreams-made-real-by-never-giving-up?.

Warner, M. (2002). *Publics and Counterpublics*. New York: Zone Books.

Watkins, S. C. (2009). *The Young and the Digital: What the Migration to Social-Network Sites, Games, and Anytime, Anywhere Media Means for Our Future*. Boston: Beacon Press.

Wischenbart, R. (2019). The Business of Books 2019: Publishing in the Age of the Attention Economy. White paper held at Frankfurter Buchmesse 2019.

Wood, H. (2019). Margaret Atwood Sheds Light on Hacker's Efforts to Steal the Testaments. *The Bookseller*, September 10. www.thebookseller .com/news/margaret-atwood-discusses-attempted-cyber-theft-testaments-1079281.

Wood, H. (2021). Booker Remains World's Most Visible Literary Prize, Research Shows. *The Bookseller*, December 22. www.thebookseller .com/news/booker-remains-most-visible-literary-prize-research-shows-1296568#.

Yee, K. (2022). Good News Alert: Amazon is Closing its Physical Bookstores. *Literary Hub*, March 2. https://lithub.com/good-news-alert-amazon-is-closing-its-physical-bookstores/.

Acknowledgments

Our interdisciplinary collaboration began in 2020 when Corinna Norrick-Rühl joined the WWU Münster and the Collaborative Research Center "Law and Literature" funded by the German Research Foundation (DFG SFB 1385 2019–2023); for Caroline Koegler, it is a particular joy that Corinna joined the sub-project "Literature and the Market" (A02) that they both co-lead alongside Professor Dr. Petra Pohlmann (Antitrust Law) and Professor Dr. Gernot Sieg (Economics). We are grateful to the German Research Foundation and Professor Dr. Klaus Stierstorfer, spokesperson of the SFB 1385, for providing an inspiring and supportive research framework that truly invites and fosters interdisciplinary exchange. The DFG SFB 1385 also supported the publication via open access. In addition, the following student assistants from the DFG SFB 1385 provided research assistance and assisted with copy editing and formatting during the writing process (in alphabetical order): Chandni Ananth, Kira Beyer, and Mathilda Dick.

We have incurred both individual and professional debts while writing this Element. When we pitched the Element, the pandemic was only just beginning, and we are grateful to the series editor Samantha Rayner as well as the Strand editors Laura Dietz and Rachel Noorda for their patience with us as we worked on the manuscript. We are also grateful to our colleagues in the DFG SFB 1385, in particular Professor Dr. Petra Pohlmann and Professor Dr. Gernot Sieg, for valuable conversations and discussions, which helped shape the direction of this Element in its early stages. Bethany Thomas and Adam Hooper at Cambridge University Press have been wonderful to work with throughout the preparation of the manuscript. Thanks are also due to Malini Soupramanian and the team at Integra for their management of the production of the Element. We would also like to thank the anonymous peer reviewers, who gave us very valuable feedback on this project, and we only hope that we have done their comments justice in our final version.

Caroline would like to additionally thank her family for continuing in their lovely and amazing ways – all through the lockdowns and beyond. She is also immensely grateful that daycare and grandparents are continuing to help her and her partner to work, think, and realize projects that matter to them professionally. Further, she counts herself lucky that, in Corinna Norrick-Rühl, she has found a fantastic collaborator whose brilliance, enthusiasm, and kindness have been greatly enriching, making the trespassing across the boundaries between literary studies and book studies an absolute treat.

Corinna would like to add these thank yous: At WWU, I would like to express my gratitude to Birgit Hötker-Bolte and my MA students in the seminar "Between Bibliodiversity and 'Difference': Books as Commodities" (summer term 2021). At home, despite the collapse of work spaces and home spaces in the pandemic, a robust support system has enabled me to keep writing and thinking. Special thanks go to our daycare center as well as to my kids' ever-present and supportive grandparents Petra and Neal Norrick and Ruth and Karl Rühl. Throughout, Timo Rühl makes it all not only possible but worthwhile. Above all, however, my thanks are due to Caroline Koegler, whom I have learned so much from over the course of this collaboration – a collaboration that has been a source of joy in these uncertain times.

Cambridge Elements ⁼

Publishing and Book Culture

SERIES EDITOR

Samantha Rayner
University College London

Samantha Rayner is Professor of Publishing and Book Cultures
at UCL. She is also Director of UCL's Centre for Publishing,
co-Director of the Bloomsbury CHAPTER (Communication
History, Authorship, Publishing, Textual Editing and
Reading) and co-Chair of the Bookselling Research Network.

ASSOCIATE EDITOR

Leah Tether
University of Bristol

Leah Tether is Professor of Medieval Literature and Publishing
at the University of Bristol. With an academic background in
medieval French and English literature and a professional
background in trade publishing, Leah has combined her
expertise and developed an international research profile in
book and publishing history from manuscript to digital.

About the Series

This series aims to fill the demand for easily accessible, quality texts available for teaching and research in the diverse and dynamic fields of Publishing and Book Culture. Rigorously researched and peer-reviewed Elements will be published under themes, or 'Gatherings'. These Elements should be the first check point for researchers or students working on that area of publishing and book trade history and practice: we hope that, situated so logically at Cambridge University Press, where academic publishing in the UK began, it will develop to create an unrivalled space where these histories and practices can be investigated and preserved.

Cambridge Elements ≡

Publishing and Book Culture
The Business of Publishing

Gathering Editor: Rachel Noorda
Dr. Rachel Noorda is the Director of Publishing at Portland
State University. Dr. Noorda is a researcher of twenty-first
century book studies, particularly on topics of entrepreneurship,
marketing, small business, national identity, and international
publishing.

ELEMENTS IN THE GATHERING

A full series listing is available at: www.cambridge.org/EPBC

Printed in the United States
by Baker & Taylor Publisher Services